PUSH!

Birthing The Seed Of Purpose In You

Angeline L. Williams

PUSH!

Birthing The Seed Of Purpose In You

Copyright © 2021 Angeline L. Williams
ISBN-13: 978-1-7325258-3-2

Published by Redemption Books
www.redemptbooks.com

All rights reserved. No portion of this publication may be reproduced, stored in a retrieval system, or transmitted in any form or by any means, electronic, mechanical, photocopy, recording, scanning, or other except for brief quotations in printed reviews, without written permission of the publisher.

This title and other titles by author are available for quantity discounts. Visit www.angelinelwilliams.com.

Book Design: Williams DocuPrep
www.williamsdocuprep.com

Unless otherwise noted, scripture quotations are taken from the New King James Version®. Copyright © 1982 by Thomas Nelson. Used by permission. All rights reserved. Scripture quotations marked (NLT) are taken from the Holy Bible, New Living Translation, copyright © 1996, 2004, 2007, 2013, 2015 by Tyndale House Foundation. Used by permission. Scripture quotations marked (ESV) are taken from The Holy Bible, English Standard Version®, copyright © 2001 by Crossway, a publishing ministry of Good News Publishers. Used by permission. Scripture quotations marked NIV are taken from The Holy Bible, New International Version ®. Copyright© 1973, 1978, 1984, 2011 by Biblica, Inc.™. Used by permission of Zondervan.

Table of Contents

Table of Contents 1

Preface 3

Dedication 6

Eternity 7

Introduction 18

It Starts With A Seed 26

   The Parable Of The Sower (Luke 8) 28

By Faith 38

   Faith To Obey 41

   The Faith Of Abraham 47

   Caleb's Faith 60

   Supernatural Living 67

Praying Through to Birth 75

Relationship 78

Fasting 85

The Battle For Your Purpose... 88

The Battle For Your Mind..96

Casting Down Imaginations 101

No Weapon Will Prosper!... 105

Fight Spiritual Battles, the Jesus Way.................. 107

The Birthing Process 117

Conception and Implantation 118

The Holy Spirit Will Come Upon You 123

During Pregnancy 127

The Transition... 134

Encouragement In The Labor Room....................... 138

King David.. 139

Joseph... 143

It's Going To Be Alright... 148

Final Thoughts.. 155

About The Author 161

Preface

It was a little after three a.m. when God woke me up and began to speak about birthing the Seed of Purpose and His promises in my life. I didn't realize it then, but I can clearly see it now that God has given me a book series on the power of His Word in our lives. I've noticed that many in the Body of Christ are hearing the same things that I am hearing.

We are in the last days and the world is waiting in earnest expectation on us—the children of God to be revealed (Romans 8:19). God is moving and shifting things suddenly, and the Body of Christ must be alert and ready to move with Him. Every day, we must walk in constant faith and expectancy. We must cooperate with Him, and speak what He speaks so that His will can be done in the Earth.

In the first book of this series, *"Put The Word In Your Mouth,"* I talk about the power of God's Word in our mouth. In the book *"Promises, Promises, God Always Keeps His Promises,"* I talk about how to cultivate a deeper relationship with God, and I guide you through praying the scriptures, so you can walk in the victory that belongs to you.

Now in *"Push! Birthing The Seed of Purpose In You,"* I talk about bringing forth the purpose that God has embedded in you before He formed you in your mother's womb. You can accomplish all that God created you to do. All three, or any of these books, will help you walk into and fulfill your divine destiny.

I did not know that there were so many books on this subject until I finished writing it. I didn't read any of them to compare with what I wrote, since what I wrote is by inspiration of the Holy Spirit as God gave it to me. I published it, believing that God will put this book into the hands of every person who needs it.

As I began to put pen to paper, intense warfare came against me with the intent of distracting me. The attack of Satan assures me that this is no ordinary book, but rather a tool that the Holy Spirit will use to break yokes, lead you to breakthrough, and help propel you into God's purpose for your life.

As you walk with me through *"Push! Birthing The Seed Of Purpose In You,"* I trust that something is said to ignite the fire in you and inspire you to move ahead with greater determination toward the purpose to which the Lord has called you. Just like with a normal baby delivery, birthing your Divine Seed of Purpose may not be easy, but I promise, it is worth it. God has something to say to us in the Body of Christ today, and He is speaking through His Word. So, let's get to it.

> *"But when the fullness of the time had come, God sent forth His Son, born of a woman, born under the law,"* —Galatians 4:4

Dedication

I give honor, and glory to God, who has inspired every page of this book. I dedicate this book to every person who recognizes that they have a God appointed destiny; to those who are not satisfied with where they are, and to those whose hearts keep pushing them to strive for more.

Eternity

Many people don't like to think of eternity. They try to shut their eyes to it, but the fact remains that there is an eternity. Ecclesiastes 3:11 says that *"God has set eternity in the hearts of men."* So, whether they acknowledge it, or not, every person has a sense that there is more than just this life.

Unless we turn a deaf ear to it, we all hear an inner voice reminding us, calling out to us about where we will spend eternity. Will we spend it with God in Heaven, or without God in Hell? It doesn't matter if you've told yourself that there is no heaven or hell, your spirit knows they exist. So, where are you going to spend eternity? In fact, Jesus Christ made it very clear that a person's relationship with God in this present life determines his destiny in the life to come (Matthew 19:16-26; 7:13-23).

When I hear that someone has passed on from this life, the first thoughts that come to my mind are, "Were they ready to meet God?" Was their name written in the Lamb's Book of Life? Did they know Jesus? When I think about my family and friends, the first thought that comes to my mind is, "Are they ready?" Is their name written in the Lamb's Book of Life? Do they know Jesus? So, before we go further, when was the last time you thought about eternity? Do you know where you will spend eternity? There are two different states of eternity. One is with God, and one is without God.

The times we live in are uncertain! Each one of us has an appointed time to die. Eternity is coming for you, whether you want it to or not. None of us knows when that time will come. Some of us have years to live, some have days, and some have hours, but we don't know how long we have. Even if a doctor has said you have a few months, he doesn't know either. Only God knows. So, I ask you, where will you spend eternity? Are you ready to meet God? Have you been born again?

Why does a person need to be born again? In the Garden of Eden, God told Adam and Eve that if they ate of the tree of the knowledge of good and evil, it would result in death.

"And the LORD God commanded the man, saying, 'You may surely eat of every tree of the garden, but of the tree of the knowledge of good and evil you shall not eat, for in the day that you eat of it you shall surely die.'"

Up to that point, death did not exist. After this, humans lived for hundreds of years (Genesis 5). As time has progressed, our lifespan has shortened. "You shall surely die" means a continuous state of death which begins with spiritual death and continues throughout life as our body continues to deteriorate, and ends in physical death.

Spiritual death resulted in Adam's separation from God (Genesis 3:8). Immediately, he knew that he was now separated from God. When God came to fellowship with him, as He did every day, he hid from God. When God questioned him about his actions, he tried to blame Eve for his sin (Genesis 3:12).

Sadly, as the representative of the human race, when Adam sinned, the entire world was affected. A seed always reproduces after its own kind. In Genesis 1:26, we read that God made man in His own image, saying, *"Let Us make man in Our image."* The Spirit of God lived in man. But in Genesis 5:3, it says that when Adam had lived 130 years, he fathered a son in his own likeness, after his image, and named him Seth. Look at that!

A radical change had taken place within man after the sin of Adam. Man went from being made in the image of God with the Spirit of God living inside him to man being created in his own image. As he procreated, his sin nature was passed down to the next generation.

Someone asked me how a baby can be born a sinner. Babies are innocent because they have not done any sinful deeds, but they are born with the sin nature that was passed down from Adam. In Romans 5:12, Paul explains that sin entered the world through one man (Adam), and death through sin, and in this way, death came to all people. As descendants of Adam, the sin nature was passed down to us.

Imagine if you took an uncontaminated glass of water and added a drop of deadly poison to it. That poison will permeate the whole glass of water. That is what sin has done to humanity. Since the Spirit of God is no longer in man, sin has permeated man's entire being. That is to say, his intellect, affections, and will are all tainted by sin.

The Bible says in Proverbs 22:15, *"Folly is bound up in the heart of a child . . ."* King David in Psalm 51:5 said, *"Surely I was sinful at birth, sinful from the time my mother conceived me."* This does not mean that his mother bore him out of wedlock. It means that his mother inherited a sin nature from her parents, and they from their parents, and so on. David inherited a sin nature from his parents, as we all do. Even if we live the best lives possible, we are still sinners because of inherited sin.

No one has to teach a child to lie or be selfish. "I didn't do it," or "it's mine," they say. Where does this come from? We may not want to acknowledge it, and it may seem unfair, but sinful behavior comes naturally to babies because they inherit a sin nature from their parents. In fact, we have to teach children not to steal, not to lie, the value of telling the truth, sharing, and so on. If you've had children, you know that this is true.

The good news is that Adam's sin did not surprise God. Before the foundation of the world, God made provision for humanity to return to Him. He sent His Son, Jesus Christ, into the world to pay the penalty for our sin on the cross through His death and resurrection. We may not have a choice about being born in sin, but we do have a choice about remaining in sin. Romans 5:19 says, *"For as by one man's disobedience many were made sinners, so also by one Man's obedience many will be made righteous."*

"To all who receive him, to those who believed in his name, he gave the right to become children of God not born of natural descent, but born of God."—John 1:12–13

The apostle Paul in Ephesians 2:1 says, *"And you He made alive, who were dead in trespasses and sins."* Only those who are born again have their sins forgiven and have a relationship with God.

Look at this conversation between Jesus and the Pharisee, Nicodemus:

> *"¹ Now there was a Pharisee, a man named Nicodemus who was a member of the Jewish ruling council. ² He came to Jesus at night and said, "Rabbi, we know that you are a teacher who has come from God. For no one could perform the signs you are doing if God were not with him." ³ Jesus replied, "Very truly I tell you, no one can see the kingdom of God unless they are born again."*
>
> *⁴ "How can someone be born when they are old?" Nicodemus asked. "Surely, they cannot enter a second time into their mother's womb to be born!" ⁵ Jesus answered, "Very truly I tell you, no one can enter the kingdom of God unless they are born of water and the Spirit. ⁶ Flesh gives birth to flesh, but the Spirit gives birth to spirit. ⁷ You should not be surprised at my saying, 'You must be born again.' ⁸ The wind blows wherever it pleases. You hear its sound, but you cannot tell where it comes from or where it is going. So, it is with everyone born of the Spirit."*
> —John 3:1-8 NIV

No matter how good you, or those around you think you are, you must be born again to connect with God. When we receive spiritual life through faith in Christ, the Bible likens it to a rebirth. It cost God a lot to make salvation possible—the blood of His own dear Son. He did it out of love. *"For God so loved the world that he gave his one and only Son, that whoever believes in him shall not perish but have eternal life"* (John 3:16).

Have you put your faith and trust in Him? If not, open your heart to Christ right now. If you are not born again, now is the time to accept Jesus Christ. None of us know when we will take our last breath and leave this earth or when Jesus will come back. We need to be ready for Jesus' return.

Jesus said in Matthew 7:22-23, *"Many will say to Me on that day, 'Lord, Lord, did we not prophesy in Your name, and in Your name cast out demons, and in Your name perform many miracles?' And then I will declare to them, 'I never knew you; depart from me, you who practice lawlessness."*

Please don't believe that:

- Believing only in God WILL save you.

- Going to church WILL save you.
- Obeying the Ten Commandments WILL save you.
- Joining a religious organization WILL save you.
- Giving money or volunteering to charity WILL save you.
- The Universe WILL save you.
- Changing your behavior WILL save you.
- Water baptism WILL save you.
- And please don't think because you are young you have time TO GET SAVED.

There is nothing we can do to make ourselves acceptable; we need God to save us. There is only one God and there is only one way to God. Jesus said in John 14:6, *"I am the way, the truth, and the life: NO MAN cometh unto the Father, but by me."*

Only the blood of Jesus cleanses the soul of man from sin. (1st John 1:7). Accepting Jesus as your

Lord and Savior is the most important decision you will ever make. It is not about a bunch of rules and regulations. That is a lie of the devil. Salvation is of the Lord, not of man. Salvation is a gift, not a reward. Salvation is by grace through faith in Christ alone (Ephesians 2:8,9).

If you do not receive the gift of salvation before you die, you will die in sin and be eternally separated from God. After death, the spirit man can only live in two places: paradise with God or hell. There is no changing your final destination after death. If you receive Him, you will be born again.

> *"But to all who did receive him, who believed in his name, he gave the right to become children of God, who were born, not of blood nor of the will of the flesh nor of the will of man, but of God."* —John 1:12-13

If you're not sure where you'll spend eternity and want to spend it in Heaven, right now, talk to God in your own way. Acknowledge that you have broken God's laws. Ask God to forgive you for your sin. Pray to God and confess your belief in Jesus Christ. Accept Him as your Lord and Savior. This is the first step in your relationship with God. You can say something like:

> *Father God, I admit that I have done things that were wrong. I am a sinner, and my sins have separated me from you. Please forgive me, and help me avoid sinning again. I believe that Your Son, Jesus Christ, died for my sins, was resurrected from the dead, is alive, and hears my prayer. I invite Jesus to become the Lord of my life. Thank you for forgiving all of my sins. By faith, I receive Your forgiveness now and declare that I want to live for you for the rest of my life. Come and fill my life with your Holy Spirit. I now depend completely on You. Amen.*

If you have prayed this prayer and meant it, you are born again. I am so glad that you made the decision to trust in Jesus. I want to personally welcome you to the Body of Christ and celebrate with you.

I would love to hear from you. Contact me on my website: www.angelinelwilliams.com, or reach out to me on Facebook: www.facebook.com/angeline.williams, and let me know of your decision.

Angeline L. Williams

Introduction

For the creation waits with eager longing for the revealing of the sons of God.—Romans 8:19 ESV

I love watching movies and reading stories about underdogs and ordinary people doing extraordinary things. They just make me feel good all over. They help me believe that no matter how insignificant I may feel, God can do something extraordinary with me. That's just the kind of God He is!

In fact, throughout the Bible, we see God choosing to release His work on the earth through ordinary people, and even those who have experienced failure. So don't say, "I'm such a failure. There is no way God is calling me to do anything." Even if you are a new Christian, God can still use you. God has a plan for your life. It's a good plan.

> *"For I know the plans I have for you," declares the Lord, "plans to prosper you and not to harm you, plans to give you a hope and a future." —* Jeremiah 29:11

God knows what He has in store for you. There's nothing in God's plan that says He intends harm or unhappiness for your life. His plans for you include prosperity, safety, hope, and the promise of a future. His plan for you is good! He is not looking for perfection from you. He is looking for trust, faith, and obedience. I want you to let that settle in your spirit. Keep that knowledge and promise in mind as you read through this book with the Holy Spirit.

When we have been called, appointed, and anointed by God for kingdom work, most of us will not fit the description that man usually looks for (1 Samuel 16:12-13). I had someone say to me that God doesn't call regular people as prophets and pastors. Who am I that God would call me? For the sake of keeping peace, I didn't say anything. I know that God called me, and I have been fervently praying for them to be saved. So, there was no need to try to convince them. I didn't say that God is God, and He calls whoever He wants to do His will, and most of the time, we are the most unlikely candidates.

I didn't mention that when God wanted to send His Son into the world to redeem the lost, He chose an ordinary young virgin named Mary to be His mother. I didn't mention how God called Moses, who was a murderer and an outlaw, to lead the nation of Israel to freedom. I said nothing about David, an adulterer who arranged for the murder of his lover's husband. I didn't mention anything about Peter, who had an anger problem and denied Jesus three times when he had the chance to defend Him. No, I didn't say all that because God has shown me that He is going to use him mightily as well. I just continue to pray and praise God for the day when His word is manifested in his life.

During the Bible days, God released His purposes through ordinary men and women, and He's still doing so today. Those of us who listen, partner with Him to do His will in the earth. What an amazing thought! We can actually partner with the all-knowing, all-powerful God to do His will on the earth. Being God's partner is more than behaving morally or doing good things to please Him. While doing these things is good, the desire of God's heart for His partners is to express Him on the earth by being His vessels.

Romans 9:22-24 says:

"[22] In the same way, even though God has the right to show his anger and his power, he is very patient with those on whom his anger falls, who are destined for destruction. [23] He does this

to make the riches of his glory shine even brighter on those to whom he shows mercy, who were prepared in advance for glory. 24 And we are among those whom he selected, both from the Jews and from the Gentiles.

A vessel is a hollow container with an opening. Its sole purpose for existing is to receive and be filled with content. We are open vessels created by God for Him to live inside and do His will in us, for us, and through us in the earth. If we don't understand this, we cannot experience all that belongs to us because of the Cross. Neither will we be able to birth the Seed of Purpose God has embedded in us. Understanding that we are to be open vessels for God to fill is key to fulfilling our purpose in the Kingdom of God.

Many times, we can get in our own way, and limit what God is trying to do in us and through us. It has been said that graveyards are filled with books never written, dreams never achieved, and life purposes never fulfilled. This is something I often tell people who come to me wanting to write and self-publish a book to encourage them not to sleep on their dream.

I hear various reasons why they haven't done it, even though they are convinced that God has called them to write and publish the book. Some say they feel they lack the skills. Some say circumstances stopped them. Others let people's discouraging words rob them of the enthusiasm to pursue their God-given vision.

Just about every person mentioned in the Bible, nearly every entertainer, entrepreneur, athlete, or anyone who has amassed any type of success has endured struggles and setbacks before their God-given dreams were realized. They had to overcome many obstacles, but each will tell you that when they pressed on, their faith increased, and they experienced many successes along the way. When you hear their stories, you see that no matter what came to stop them, the Seed of Purpose in them pushed them through.

I, too, have had my share of life's difficulties. I have faced many difficult situations, including experiencing life-threatening health events, and the loss of a child, but the vision God has given me and my faith in His Word keeps pushing me forward. The Word of God is where I go for inspiration when I'm discouraged. I've come to learn that in those times of difficulty, the temptation to quit is always present, but so is God. If we allow Him, He will use those situations to draw us into deeper fellowship with Him.

The Bible tells us that we should rejoice always and give thanks in all circumstances (1st Thessalonians 5:16-18). It took me some time before I could grasp how powerful it is to give thanks when things aren't going so well. When my strength is depleted, His Word strengthens me. When everything around me seems dark, and I can't see my way through, His Word gives me hope and lights my path. God walks by my side daily and gives me the strength to carry on. I praise Him for His faithfulness, and I praise God for His marvelous Word.

When God gives you a vision, you've got to know that God gave it to you, and if God gave it to you, He also equipped you to complete it. You must learn to prevail over the relentless battles that come to stop you from walking out your destiny. This is what we are going to talk about in this book, Push! The power in you to overcome in this relentless war that is set against your life's purpose ever coming to pass.

> *"And they overcame him by the blood of the Lamb and by the word of their testimony, and they did not love their lives to the death." —Revelation 12:11*

Angeline L. Williams

It Starts With A Seed

"The promises were spoken to Abraham and to his seed. Scripture does not say "and to seeds," meaning many people, but "and to your seed," meaning one person, who is Christ." — Galatians 3:16 NIV

God meets the needs of His people through seed. Everything you will receive from God, starts with a seed. God does not do things in the earth with a big bang, He works with a seed. In Genesis 8:22 God says, *"While the earth remains, seedtime and harvest, cold and heat, summer and winter, day and night, shall not cease."* This means that planting, giving, reaping, and receiving are eternal laws that will not change as long as the earth remains.

The Kingdom of God functions like a seed. It works on the principle of seedtime and harvest. You may have heard this about sowing and reaping money, but a seed may also be in the form of words spoken by you. Salvation and eternal life came from a seed. God sowed His only begotten Son in the earth as a seed, so you can have life. He continues to reap a harvest of sons and daughters from that seed. The Word of God is the seed that makes the Kingdom work in our lives. Understanding this is key to manifesting what Jesus has afforded you at the Cross (John 10:10).

The Parable Of The Sower (Luke 8)

> *"5 A farmer went out to sow his seed. As he was scattering the seed, some fell along the path; it was trampled on, and the birds ate it up. 6 Some fell on rocky ground, and when it came up, the plants withered because they had no moisture. 7 Other seed fell among thorns, which grew up with it and choked the plants. 8 Still other seed fell on good soil. It came up and yielded a crop, a hundred times more than was sown." When he said this, he called out, "Whoever has ears to hear, let them hear." —Luke 8:5-8*

Everyone loves a good story. Jesus was an excellent storyteller. He often used parables when He spoke. Parables are earthly stories that use common life analogies to illustrate spiritual truths. Jesus used the parable of the sower to explain different responses people have to the gospel of Jesus Christ and the Word of God. Jesus said if we don't understand the truths in the parable of the sower, we won't understand any of His other parables.

The Bible says the Word of God is a two-edged sword. It hits on both sides. The same goes with Jesus' parables. His parables delivered divine truths and judgements. The Parable of the Sower is a story most Believers in Christ are familiar with. It is the key to understanding how the Word of God functions in our lives. It tells us how we receive the Word of God, and why what He plants in us is so very important.

In this parable, Jesus uses three symbols: a Sower, seed, and soil. The Sower symbolizes God, and anyone who teaches, preaches, or shares His Word with others. The seed symbolizes the Word of God, as stated in Luke 8:11. The soil refers to the human heart, where the Word of God must be received, accepted, and nourished so it can bear fruit. Like physical seeds must remain in the ground to sprout and grow, the Word of God must abide in a heart to grow.

Let's look at what Jesus says.

"Some seed fell by the wayside; and the birds of the air came and devoured it." The birds represent Satan. This group of people didn't give much thought at all to the word planted in them, they were focused on other things. It's like the word went in one ear and

out the other. It was not kept and pondered upon, which is why Satan comes at once and takes away the Word sown in them.

When we sense God is speaking to us through a passage of Scripture, through one of His prophets, or however He gives it, we should ponder it, talk with Him about it to get its full meaning, and how it directly relates to our life.

"Some fell on stony ground, where it did not have much earth." The stony ground represents people who hear the word and respond to it initially with enthusiasm, but their interest is as shallow as thin soil among the rocks, so their enthusiasm dries up. They have no commitment to Christ, so there is no solid foundation for the Word of God to grow and mature in their heart. When difficulties or tribulations come because of the Word, it quickly falls away.

"Some seed fell among thorns; and the thorns grew up and choked it, and it yielded no crop." There can be thorns in our heart such as materialism and concern for riches, jealousy, anger, unforgiveness,

worry, what others think, and more that choke the Word, so it doesn't yield a harvest.

"But some seed fell on rich soil and produced fruit, it came up and grew and yielded a hundredfold." This is the heart of a person who is fully yielded to God's cultivation process. When the Word is planted in their heart, it is fertilized by meditating on it and talking with God about it to get its full meaning, and how it directly relates to their life.

A seed is persistent, it never gives up (Jeremiah 1:12). The Seed of Purpose God has planted in you will never stop trying to produce in you what God has planted. We've talked about how important it is to receive the Word of God, but what we do with the Word we receive is just as important. In the parable, everyone receives seed, so everyone has potential for harvest.

The Bible makes it clear that the Word of God is an incorruptible seed that will never fail. The Word of God will always produce, but you must plant the Word in your heart. The best way to plant the seed of God's Word in your heart is by spending time reading the Word (every day), meditating on the Word, and speaking the Word. This is the process of conception.

Conception cannot take place without the planting of a seed. When planted, the seed stimulates growth and development, in our relationship with the Lord. (Romans 12:2) As we nurture the seed, it becomes a part of us, and we get to the point where we believe it, then it comes out of the soil of our heart and manifests a harvest. Praying and believing for God's intervention without the seeds of conception (planting God's Word) will only lead to frustrating results.

Hearing others speak the Word is good, but it will not produce as bountiful a harvest as speaking the Word of God yourself. When you speak the word in faith concerning whatever circumstance you are facing, you are planting it. When the Word of God is planted, there will be growth and development. So, it's important that you are continually sowing the Word of God in your heart. Your healing is in that seed. Your deliverance is in that seed.

Everything grace has made available has been put in the seed of God's Word.

In the book of Jeremiah 1:5-8, God has a Word for you,

> *"5 Before I formed you in the womb, I knew you; Before you were born, I sanctified you; I ordained you a prophet to the nations." 6 Then said I: "Ah, Lord God! Behold, I cannot speak, for I am a youth." 7 But the Lord said to me: "Do not say, 'I am a youth,' For you shall go to all to whom I send you, and whatever I command you, you shall speak. 8 Do not be afraid of their faces, For I am with you to deliver you," says the Lord."*

God spoke this Word to the prophet Jeremiah, but He left it for you so that you will know that you do not simply exist, neither were you saved just to go to heaven. Before you were conceived, God decided the details of your life. That's why He brought you here.

Now let's make this verse personal, so you can see and hear what God is saying to you. Add your name in the blank line:

Before I formed you in the womb _____, I knew you. Before you were born, I sanctified you, and I ordained you for a specific purpose. Do not say, 'I can't do it,' For you shall go to all to whom I send you, and whatever I command you, you shall speak. You will fulfill your purpose _____. Do not be afraid, for I am with you," says the Lord.

We have been chosen and created with a purpose, and we have been given the grace to get the job done through Christ Jesus (Acts 4:33). David praised God in Psalms 139:16 (NLT) saying, *"You saw me before I was born. Every day of my life was recorded in your book. Every moment was laid out before a single day had passed."*

Beloved, you are a seed of God planted in the world around you, and you have an important role to play in the Kingdom of God. You were born at a specific time, placed in a specific location, with a specific assignment, for a specific duration and season. Regardless of the circumstances surrounding your birth, you were intentionally conceived in the mind of God with value and great significance.

Understanding this should help each of us celebrate our unique make up, as well as our strategic placement and function. It should help us to see that no one person is less valuable than another, and no one person is superior or inferior to others, because we are all planted by God to fulfill His divine purpose.

Your God given purpose may be different from what you've imagined. It may even seem insignificant to you, but God brought you here to complete it. It may not be clear to you yet, but you may have been sensing something is happening, changes taking place in your life that you have no control over. You may feel that your purpose is not significant enough or godly enough. However, our primary purpose in life is to direct people to Jesus, no matter what we are doing.

The Seed in you has the power to fulfill God's purpose for your life. He uniquely designed you, and He equips you daily to fulfill the purpose He has planted in you. Pray and seek God about what He has placed in you. Follow Him closely. Think big and see yourself becoming big. You were born to reign as a king or queen. Settle in your heart and mind that God didn't create you to just get by and have just enough for what you need. He is not a get by God. He is a God of breakthrough. He is a God of overflow.

God's desire is to powerfully bless and multiply His children! He is glorified when we are blessed. He wants us to live an abundant life, so we can be a blessing to others. He wants you to enjoy the things He blesses us with. He just doesn't want you to develop an improper love for them. Remember, it is the "love" of money that becomes the root of all sorts of evil, not money itself. This includes the love of things also. When you are filled with joy, you carry that joy everywhere you go.

There are people who will try to convince you that God wants you to be poor, or to have just enough. That having wealth or abundance is not of God. Ignore them! God's name is El Shaddai, which means the God of more than enough. There are so many examples in the Bible of people God made wealthy, and God can make you wealthy too if it's necessary for your purpose.

Don't let people talk you out of your blessing. God's purpose and vision for your life can be revealed to you in many ways. A lot of the time, you will feel or hear it in more than one way. With that being said, always consult with God after someone has given you a word to make sure that it is truly from God.

Angeline L. Williams

By Faith

"For we walk by faith, not by sight." —2 Corinthians 5:7

There are two different types of faith, natural and supernatural. Every person is born with natural faith. Natural faith is accepting something is true based upon natural knowledge, and things you can see, taste, hear, smell, and feel. Natural faith is accepting something is true when you have the proof or evidence for it. Natural faith says: "Except I see, except I touch, I will not believe." It says, "because you have seen, you have believed." The disciple Thomas showed natural faith. Although natural faith comes from God, it does not require faith in God or a relationship with God.

Supernatural faith is accepting something as true without any evidence or proof. It acknowledges things as if they exist, even before they happen. Hebrews 11:1 tells us that *"faith is the substance of things hoped for, the evidence of things not seen."*

One translation says, *"Now faith is the assurance (the confirmation, the title deed) of the things [we] hope for, being the proof of things [we] do not see and the conviction of their reality [faith perceiving as real fact what is not revealed to the senses]."* By standing on your faith, you have the substance of the things that you want, that you hope for, and you have the evidence of the things that you can't see at that time.

How do we get the conviction to believe? The Bible says this kind of faith is a gift of God, and it comes by hearing the Word of God (Romans 10:17). Supernatural faith supersedes natural laws. It reaches into the realm of the spirit to bring forth the fulfillment of God's promises. It brings spiritual and physical blessings.

Romans 5:2 says we have access by faith into the grace of God. If you want healing for your body, healing for your emotions, or healing in your family, you must get it by faith. Faith brings action in the earth. If you need a car, shelter, finances, a job, food, or whatever your need might be, faith is the vehicle that will manifest it from eternity to the present.

Abraham exhibited supernatural faith when he believed God's Word that he would become the father of many nations, before he had a single child. The following passage talks about men who also did great things for God through supernatural faith, and they possessed what was promised.

> *"And what more shall I say? I do not have time to tell about Gideon, Barak, Samson and Jephthah, about David and Samuel and the prophets, who through faith conquered kingdoms, administered justice, and gained what was promised; who shut the mouths of lions, quenched the fury of the flames, and escaped the edge of the sword; whose weakness was turned to strength; and who became powerful in battle and routed foreign armies."* — Hebrews 11:32-34 NIV

Faith To Obey

Faith in God and obedience to God go hand in hand. Faith is invisible, it is proven or made visible through obedience. Faith becomes perfect through obedience. When you trust someone, you'll do what they say. In essence, your faith in God and His Word can be measured through your obedience to God and His Word. I was talking with someone who said that Christianity is just a way to control the masses, and that it only works on people who are afraid of hell.

They said the Bible was written by man, and there was no way that they could believe anything a mere man has to say. They said hell is not real; it is just an idea created by religion to control people. They couldn't understand how regular people can just decide to give themselves titles as pastors, evangelists, and prophets.

As I listened, I thought, "Well, when you look at the behavior of some of us Christians, and the way some people do church, it's easy to see why some people don't believe." While it's true that the Bible says Satan, who is the god of this world, has blinded the minds of those who don't believe (2 Corinthians 4:4), the way some of us Christians think and behave has given him something to work with to deceive those around us? This is a question we should ask ourselves. We don't want or should not want to be one who turns people away from Christ rather than drawing them to Him.

As Christians, we are ambassadors for Christ, not just in church, but every day, and everywhere we go. Think about this: Scripture says that Adam and Eve were created in the image and likeness of God (Genesis 1:26-27). The word "image" in Hebrew is "tselem," which means a representation of something. The Hebrew word for "likeness," is "dmûwth," which means "resemblance." So, mankind was originally created to be a visible representation of who God is, a reflection of God's nature and character in the earth.

Therefore, we were originally created with a natural capacity for goodness, love, mercy, justice, compassion, and holiness. Sin changed all of this, and Jesus got it back for us. Jesus came to reveal to us the heavenly Father. Now with the Holy Spirit, we can continue to reflect God's image. Through Christ, God is making us more holy, working in us, making us more Christlike.

Second Corinthians 3:18 says we are being transformed into the same image from one degree of glory to another. Colossians 3:9–10 says, *"you have taken off your old self with its practices and have put on the new self, which is being renewed in knowledge in the image of its Creator."*

Second Corinthians 7:1 adds, *"Since we have these promises, beloved, let us cleanse ourselves from every defilement of body and spirit, bringing holiness to completion in the fear of God."* We will continue to be transformed all of our days.

When I understood and accepted all of this, I realized how important it is that I represent Christ well. I had to ask God to forgive me for things that I have done and said that did not represent Christ well. Maybe in your life, there have been religious leaders who've been hurtful or demeaning in some way. I encourage you to forgive them and bless them. Maybe you were one who said or did things that contributed to someone not believing in the Bible. Ask God to forgive you and then forgive yourself.

The Apostle Paul is viewed as one of the greatest men of faith. Satan constantly harassed him, but rather than end the harassment, God allowed it for Paul's benefit and ultimately ours. God used all Paul endured to keep him humble on account of the visions and revelations He shared with him.

> *"7 And lest I should be exalted above measure by the abundance of the revelations, a thorn in the flesh was given to me, a messenger of Satan to buffet me, lest I be exalted above measure. 8 Concerning this thing I pleaded with the Lord three times that it might depart from me. 9 And He said to me, "My grace is sufficient for you, for My strength is made perfect in weakness." Therefore, most gladly I will rather boast in my infirmities, that the power of Christ may rest upon me."* —2 Corinthians 12:7-9

Buffet or buffeting is a continuous nonstop action coming against you to hinder your progress and to curtail your activity. It is like being struck with the fist continuously. Paul says when he and his team got to Macedonia, they were weary and troubled on every side. Outside was conflict, inside was fear, but God, who comforts the downcast, comforted them by sending Titus (2 Corinthians 7:5-6).

Many people think Paul's thorn in the flesh was some sickness that God sent to keep him humble, so they submit to sickness, and other things from Satan thinking it is pleasing to God. However, James 4:7 tells us to, *"Submit yourselves therefore to God. Resist the devil, and he will flee from you."* We must submit to God and use our faith to fight against the things the devil brings to distract us. We must resist what causes us to doubt God and His Word so we can walk in the victory that belongs to us.

God told Paul His strength is made perfect in weakness, not infirmity. Jesus took care of sickness and infirmity at the Cross. He healed all manner of sickness and disease (physical and mental) while on earth, but not one time do we see Jesus delivering someone from persecution. In fact, the Bible tells us to expect persecution.

> *"Beloved, do not be surprised at the fiery trial when it comes upon you to test you, as though something strange were happening to you."* — 1 Peter 4:12

Paul asked the Lord three times to remove the thorn or persecution from him, and finally the Lord told him, *"My grace is sufficient."* That was enough for Paul. He moved forward in faith, trusting that God would give him the strength, and the power to endure whatever was ahead. Whatever came, He obeyed the voice of the Lord. Paul's ultimate goal was to be conformed to the image of Christ, and to help others do the same (1 Corinthians 11:1). He believed that no matter what happened, it would somehow benefit the Kingdom of God and end in good for him.

It is my prayer that you and I will trust that if God allows any obstacle, persecution, or trouble in our life, He has a purpose for it. That He will give us the strength, the power, and the faith to endure. That we will obey the voice of the Lord no matter what we face.

The Faith Of Abraham

Abraham, the "Father of Faith," is another person who can teach us how to have faith enough to obey through the birthing of the Seed of Promise in us. He shows us that faith means trusting God's Word enough to risk living by it. Both Abraham and

Sarah are great examples of living between the promise and the fulfillment of the promise. In the Bible, he is honored for his obedience (Romans 4:16).

> *"8 By faith Abraham obeyed when he was called to go out to a place that he was to receive as an inheritance. And he went out, not knowing where he was going. 9 By faith he went to live in the land of promise, as in a foreign land, living in tents with Isaac and Jacob, heirs with him of the same promise. 10 For he was looking forward to the city that has foundations, whose designer and builder is God.*
>
> *11 By faith Sarah herself received power to conceive, even when she was past the age, since she considered him faithful who had promised. 12 Therefore from one man, and him as good as dead, were born descendants as many as the stars of heaven and as many as the innumerable grains of sand by the seashore.*
>
> *13 These all died in faith, not having received the things promised, but having seen them and greeted them from afar, and having acknowledged that they were strangers and exiles on the*

earth. ¹⁴ For people who speak thus make it clear that they are seeking a homeland. ¹⁵ If they had been thinking of that land from which they had gone out, they would have had opportunity to return. ¹⁶ But as it is, they desire a better country, that is, a heavenly one. Therefore, God is not ashamed to be called their God, for he has prepared for them a city.

¹⁷ By faith Abraham, when he was tested, offered up Isaac, and he who had received the promises was in the act of offering up his only son, ¹⁸ of whom it was said, "Through Isaac shall your offspring be named." ¹⁹ He considered that God was able even to raise him from the dead, from which, figuratively speaking, he did receive him back." —Hebrews 11:8-19

Apostle Paul wrote, *"Abraham believed God, and it was credited to him as righteousness"* (Romans 4:3). When I read Abraham's story in Genesis, I see him as an example of humility, faith, and fear. I see humility when, although he was the older family member and had the right to the best land, he let Lot have his choice to avoid strife. I see humility when he risked his life and goes to battle to rescue Lot. It was fear that led Abraham to deceive Pharaoh about the true identity of his wife; but His faith to obey God is what I see the most and what I want to talk about.

Abram was around 75 years old when God called him to leave his home and family and go to a strange land. *"12 Now the Lord had said to Abram: "Get out of your country, from your family and from your father's house, to a land that I will show you. 2 I will make you a great nation; I will bless you and make your name great; and you shall be a blessing. 3 I will bless those who bless you, and I will curse him who curses you; and in you all the families of the earth shall be blessed" (Genesis 12:1-3).* In faith, Abram went out from the country of the Chaldeans and settled in Haran.

Having a son in those days was very important to a man, and it still is today. It was especially important to Abram because God said, *"I will make you a great nation."* Years went by without the fulfillment of this part of the promise. How could he become a great nation without a son to carry on his legacy? Like many of us, Abram grew fearful that the promise of God would not come to pass.

Since Abram and his wife were both quite old, they convinced themselves that there was no way that they could conceive a child. So, Sarai, Abram's wife, presented her husband with a plan for Hagar, her Egyptian maid, to serve as what we call today a surrogate mother to carry a child for her. Abram agreed. They took the matter of trying to fulfill God's promise into their own hands. Sarai loved her husband so much that she set it up for him to have a son by another woman because she couldn't.

She took Hagar and gave her to her husband to be his wife, and she conceived a son. Imagine the strength it took for her to do that. The plan was that when the child was born, it would be Sarai's son, not Hagar's. However, when Hagar saw that she had conceived, she began to look upon Sarai with disdain.

Instead of getting upset with Abraham for trying to fulfill the covenant himself, God gave Abraham a mental picture of what was to come. God took him outside and told him to look up at the stars and promised to make his descendants as the number of stars in the sky. Abram is now 99 years old, and any hope of having a son by Sarai seemed impossible. God appeared to him to reiterate His covenant promise to him:

> "*¹ When Abram was ninety-nine years old, the Lord appeared to him and said, "I am God Almighty; walk before me faithfully and be blameless. ² Then I will make my covenant between me and you and will greatly increase your numbers."*
>
> *³ Abram fell facedown, and God said to him, ⁴ "As for me, this is my covenant with you: You will be the father of many nations. ⁵ No longer will you be called Abram; your name will be Abraham, for I have made you a father of many nations. ⁶ I will make you very fruitful; I will make nations of you, and kings will come from you.*
>
> *⁷ I will establish my covenant as an everlasting covenant between me and you and your descendants after you for the generations to come, to be your God and the God of your descendants*

after you. ⁸ The whole land of Canaan, where you now reside as a foreigner, I will give as an everlasting possession to you and your descendants after you; and I will be their God."— Genesis 17:1-8 NIV

God loves you! Your mistakes don't surprise Him. He will help you see what you need to see, and hear what you need to hear to help you trust Him. No matter how some people might try to tell you, they just jumped right into faith, it did not happen. The faith to obey God happens over time. God's first words to Abraham about a new homeland for his offspring began in Genesis 12.

It was 24 years, and after the birth of Ishmael, before God told Abraham and his wife Sarah that they would be the parents of the promised child (Genesis 17:15-16). All those years, God never stopped communicating, reassuring, and reminding Abraham of His promises. Sometimes, what God promises us may seem so far out of our reach, and we laugh like Abraham did, but God always keeps His promises.

God did just as He prophesied, and Sarah gave birth to Isaac. Then, God tested Abraham and told him to take Isaac and sacrifice him on the altar. God had prepared Abraham for this and had given him the grace to do it. Over the years, God revealed himself many times to Abraham. He used Abraham's life experiences to build him into a man of faith. Through his successes and failures, God helped him cultivate the faith to obey, to the point of sacrificing his own son. He'd learned the character of God, and it was settled in his heart that God would keep His promise; that He would do what He said He would do. That is what He is doing with us. Cultivating in us the faith to obey.

Abraham rose early in the morning to make the sacrifice. He took two of his young men and his son Isaac and headed to the place God had told him to go to and perform the sacrifice. When they reached the mountain, Abraham saw the spot where God had told him to perform the sacrifice. He spoke his faith by saying to his servants, "Stay here with the donkey, and I and the lad will go over there, worship, and return to you."

He took Isaac and the items for sacrifice and headed up into the mountains. Abraham again spoke his faith when his son Isaac asked, "Where is the lamb for the offering?" Abraham said, "My son, God will provide for Himself the lamb for a burnt offering." Just as he was about to slay his son, God called to Abraham and said, "Do not lay your hand on the boy or do anything to him, for now I know that you fear God, seeing you have not withheld your son, your only son, from me." Abraham lifted up his eyes and looked, and behold, behind him was a ram, caught in a thicket by his horns. Abraham took the ram and offered it up as a burnt offering instead of his son. All of this took place on Mount Moriah. Moriah means bitterness.

Some of our experiences are very bitter, and strong faith is needed to believe that God will somehow bring good out of them. Like Abraham, we must accept God's plan and move forward, trusting in His promise, even if there is apprehension. Sometimes you are going to have to go through some stuff, to get to your stuff. And while you're going through, it may look like things can't possibly work out, but good will always come, especially when there's steadfast obedience. The faith of God will give you the strength to keep going.

I can only imagine what Abraham was truly experiencing on the inside as he was just about to slay his son. When God told me that He was taking my daughter home with Him, I didn't want to accept it. I immediately rebuked the voice that spoke to me. Then, like thunder that exploded inside me, God said, "Nothing can thwart my plan." The voice of God literally felt like thunder exploding on the inside of me. I've heard God's voice sound happy, sad, and excited, but this was the first time it shook the inside of me like a thunder roar. Then I had to repent and accept God's plan.

So, God was pleased and told Abraham, because of your obedience, your seed is going to be many, and cover the earth like all the stars you see every night. As much as the grains of sand are on the earth, your family is going to be that big. I am going to see to it that you have everything that you need and forever and ever will your family produce. This is a time I imagine God was excited as He spoke (Genesis 22:15-18).

Abraham had the faith, the strength, and the grace to obey God when He wanted him to do something he did not want to do. He had the faith, the strength, and the grace to obey God when he didn't know what was going to happen. Would you agree that what God called Abraham to do takes extraordinary strength and courage? This type of courage and strength is far above any human strength we can muster up. It is supernatural and can only come from God.

God gave Abraham the grace he needed to sustain him through what he was going through. God has given you the grace you need to sustain you through everything that will come your way as well. Everything God asks you to do, He will supply the means to do it. Because of Abraham's obedience, he was blessed tremendously. He received the promise and the reward. It will be the same for you. Your obedience moves you to your reward.

Yes, you must have faith, but you also must use your faith, and you must speak the faith that you have. Faith is believing in your heart; obedience is acting on what you believe. Walking around talking about faith and not doing anything with it will not benefit you. Do you have the faith and the courage to obey God when He tells you to do something, no matter how impossible it looks?

In Mark 4:40, because of the storm that rose up, the disciples were fearful, and they woke Jesus up from His nap. "Lord, don't you see we are about to drown here? Wake up and do something!" Jesus got up and asked, "Why are you so fearful? How is it that you have no faith?" Then He spoke peace to the storm.

In Mark chapter five, Jesus says, "Be not afraid. Only believe." Faith works based on what you believe. If you believe something will never happen, you are absolutely correct. If you believe God's going to take care of this, you are absolutely correct.

Abraham had to work through the process. He had to gather the wood. He had to tell Sarah I've got to do this. He had to travel up into the mountain, and he had to go through the trauma of preparing to burn his son. He had to be obedient and work his faith. May we all have the faith to be obedient.

Waiting on God can be hard, but we can't say we have faith in God and then sit back and wait and complain. Saying, "God, I've been waiting three weeks. When are You going to do something? When are You going to do what You said You would do God?" That is not faith. God's Word is a defensive weapon. When things get so bad that you want to scream, hit something, or throw something, use your defensive weapon

When it comes to fulfilling the purpose that God has for your life, age is just a number. There is no such thing as you're too old or too young with God. Abraham was 100 and Sarah was 90 when Isaac was born. Joseph was only 17; David was practically a child; Shadrach, Meshach, and Abednego were teenagers. What about the young boy who gave up his lunch that Jesus used to feed the 5,000?

Caleb's Faith

Birthing the promise God has placed inside of us may sometimes seem as impossible as Israel's situation. How did Caleb develop such faith that he saw the situation differently? In Exodus chapter six, God spoke to Moses saying,

> "I am the Lord. I appeared to Abraham, to Isaac, and to Jacob, as God Almighty, but by my name the Lord, I did not make myself known to them. I also established my covenant with them to give them the land of Canaan, the land in which they lived as sojourners. Moreover, I have heard the groaning of the people of Israel whom the Egyptians hold as slaves, and I have remembered my covenant." (Exodus 6:2-5 – ESV)

God remembered His covenant with Abraham, to Isaac, and to Jacob, and it was time to deliver. In His mighty power, God delivered about three million people out of Egypt, but only two of those people, Joshua, and Caleb, were allowed to go into the Promised Land. God saw something particularly different about Caleb that made Him say, *"But My servant Caleb, because he has a different spirit in him and has followed Me fully, I will bring [him] into the land where he went, and his descendants shall inherit it"* (Numbers 14:24).

It wasn't that Caleb had extraordinary courage, zeal, or determination. Each of the 12 spies had these qualities, which is why they were chosen. So, what was different about Caleb? Let's ponder this for a moment. Caleb spent the first 40 years of his life as a slave in Egypt. He grew up hearing about God's promise to his ancestor Abraham (Genesis 15:7-15), that God would powerfully deliver Israel from oppression and bring them into the land He had promised. I imagine that as he saw the miracles of the plagues being carried out, he got excited because he knew the time had come for deliverance.

Then he watched the powerful hand of God miraculously free the nation of Israel from slavery. Imagine how happy they all must have been to finally be free and on their way. Then, God led them straight toward the Red Sea, not around it, but right up to its shore. They were overcome with fear and helplessness. Israel had the Egyptian army chasing them, and they had come to the borders of the sea and had nowhere left to go. They cried out to Moses, saying, "Because there were no graves in Egypt, have you taken us away to die in the wilderness?"

Have you ever had a time when it seemed as if your back was against the wall? When you look to the left, you see trouble. When you look to the right, there is trouble. Behind you, there is trouble, and you can't see your way clear to move forward. What are you supposed to do in a situation like this? You trust God that He will honor His Word as He has done so many times before. I've learned that it is at this time, in the darkest of night that God performs the miraculous. He drives back the sea and makes a way for you. So do not fear. Do not allow discouragement to linger when impossible circumstances close in around you.

God is always working to get you to birth what He placed inside you, but you must trust Him. Caleb saw the Red Sea split in two, and the ground that had been covered by water become bone dry. He watched all night long as nearly three million people walked across an ocean floor on dry land with a wall of water on their right and on their left to freedom (Exodus 14:21-22).

It was time for the next phase of the covenant God spoke to Abraham to manifest, and there was nothing that could stop it. This is just like when a woman is in full labor. That baby is coming, and no one can stop it. She is going to have to push through the pain to get that baby out. Caleb believed God and took Him at His word. He was certain that the mission could be accomplished. God said He had given them the land, and if God had given them the land, it was God's will that they occupy it. If it was God's will that they occupy it, then God would help them take possession of it.

Sometimes it is easy to see obstacles as giants, and we feel helpless to do anything about them. But make up your mind, you either have big problems and a small God, or you have a big God and small problems. Caleb trusted in God's faithfulness to keep His promises. When obstacles stand in your way, stand on what God said, and be ready to overcome them.

Joshua and Caleb saw the same land, and the same giants as the other ten, but they saw victory and the others saw defeat. Joshua and Caleb saw blessings, the others saw the barriers. Why is it that different people have different reactions to the same reality? The ten spies give us a clue. They said, *"we were like grasshoppers in our own sight, and so we were in their sight"* (Numbers 13:33). They saw things as they were in their own eyes, not as what God said.

Do you feel like a grasshopper in comparison to the vision, the dream, or the call God has given you? Thoughts can hold you like a vise and keep you from the truth. Satan and his imps bring thousands of thoughts to our minds. These thoughts bring fear, and if they take root in our mind, we will speak those thoughts out. When this happens, what was once an accusing voice has now become your voice repeating what Satan says, rather than what God says. The spirit of fear has crushed more Christians than any other weapon Satan throws at them.

Do you see the obstacles in your Promised Land? What you see, what you think and what you say can slow down or accelerate or even prevent your breakthroughs from coming to pass. Think about the vision, the promise God has spoken over you. Look beyond the facts and look with the eyes of faith.

Through these stories I hear God saying,

"If I have promised something to you, I have also provided a way for you to obtain it. You can choose to trust and believe this beyond what your physical eyes can see, or you can choose to let fear, doubt and unbelief determine what and who you will believe. If you choose the latter, you tie my hands and there is nothing I can do, for you have chosen to wander in a wilderness of fear-based faith, and you will never inherit what I've promised. Until you decide to follow my way, you're destined to wander in the wilderness that you've chosen for yourself."

Abraham and Lot were both saved men. Lot was saved, not for his own sake, but for Abraham's (Genesis 19:29, 2 Peter 2:7-8). His salvation was not due to his faithfulness, but because Abraham interceded for him. Both men went to heaven, but they took different paths. Lot walked by sight; Abraham walked by faith. You must envision the promise before you can take possession of it.

Sometimes it may seem as if things are pressing in on you from all sides. During these times, it can be difficult to walk by faith, but God will give you the grace and strength to get through it. As I look back over some of the trials that I've been through, it seems as if I have been buffeted like Paul. Since I was a little girl, the enemy has been trying to destroy my destiny.

When I moved to Atlanta from Miami, and even more so when I realized and accepted the call on my life, there has been opposition at every turn. Many times, I've wanted to turn around and run back to Miami, and even did once, which turned out not to be good. Even still, today I had to deal with intense buffeting. What I've come to understand is that God has been cultivating in me the faith to obey His voice, and the faith to endure the next phase of life's challenges that will come with the next stage of the journey or purpose.

Many Believers in Christ are under buffeting today, so I want to talk a little about how Paul handled being buffeted and how to cultivate the faith needed to obey God's voice, and the faith to endure the next phase of life's challenges. When we put our trust in God, we'll accomplish much more than we ever dreamed possible. What is the land you are trying to conquer? Your finances? Your physical health? Marriage and family relationships? Your mental health and emotions? Whatever it may be, *"Every place where you set your foot will be yours"* (Deuteronomy 11:24). Halleluiah! That's a seed! Seedtime and harvest remains! He that hath an ear let him hear... Accept nothing less than victory.

Supernatural Living

He who says he abides in Him ought himself also to walk just as He walked. (1 John 2:6)

The natural man lives by what he sees through his physical eyes. His emotions, thoughts, and actions are all processed through what he sees through his physical eyes. Believers in Christ, although we live in a physical body, are spiritual beings. We live by faith, not by sight (2 Corinthians 5:7). The Seed of Purpose in you is supernatural. Its intent is to bear fruit for the Kingdom of God. This is your destiny. Therefore, it is crucial that you understand how to live in the supernatural realm on the earth.

Do you see yourself as someone God can use to release miracles, signs, and wonders on the earth? Or do you think this is reserved only for church leaders? When you hear the word supernatural, what do you think of? Is it something spooky?

God's supernatural power is natural to Him. It is part of His character, but to some people it is supernatural. Many of us have experienced the supernatural power of God at one time or another, but as Believers (spiritual beings), we are supposed to live in the supernatural realm. Our life is supposed to be a supernatural life.

Unfortunately, unbelief causes many Christians to feel disconnected from the supernatural. Even though they've read about the miracles Jesus and the apostles of the early church performed, even though they see God using people today, they can't imagine God using them in the same way.

To some people, Holy Ghost manifestations are spooky and scary, especially for babies in Christ who didn't grow up in church. Some believe healing, deliverance, raising the dead, and other supernatural manifestations were limited to the apostles of the Bible. However, if Jesus had limited the works of the Holy Spirit to the first apostles, then the Great Commission would also be limited to them. Christianity would have ended with them. There would be no Christians today. Jesus said, in Mark chapter 16,

> *"15 And He said to them, "Go into all the world and preach the gospel to every creature. 16 He who believes and is baptized will be saved; but he who does not believe will be condemned. 17 And these signs will follow those who believe: In My name they will cast out demons; they will speak with new tongues; 18 they will take up serpents; and if they drink anything deadly, it will by no means hurt them; they will lay hands on the sick, and they will recover." 19 So then, after the Lord had spoken to them, He was received*

up into heaven, and sat down at the right hand of God. 20 And they went out and preached everywhere, the Lord working with them and confirming the word through the accompanying signs. Amen."

This passage shows us that the prerequisite for working with Jesus to do the supernatural is to believe. It also shows us that the Lord will confirm the Word of God with signs and wonders whenever it is preached by whoever believes, not just the apostles. No matter how ordinary you think you are, you are special to God. He has chosen you, just as He chose the many men and women in the Bible to perform supernatural things on earth for the Kingdom. Their stories reveal what we are able to do through the power of God. If God uses one person in that way, He will use us as well. Jesus Christ is the same yesterday, today, and forevermore. God does not change.

Do you believe it? Do you see yourself as someone God can use to release miracles, signs, and wonders on the earth? God has given us everything we need to live the supernatural life. We have forgiveness of sins. We have the Holy Spirit indwelling us; we have God's Word; and we have the authority of Jesus and His name.

God has given us everything we need for life and godliness (2 Peter 1:3). Unfortunately, many don't understand what we have, who we are, and why we are here. When we confess Jesus Christ as Savior and Lord, He comes into our heart and gives us new life. Our old nature passes away, and we become a new creation, with God's supernatural nature and Spirit inside of us.

It is written in 1st John 3:2, *"Beloved, now are we the sons of God, and it doth not yet appear what we shall be: but we know that, when he shall appear, we shall be like him; for we shall see him as he is."* We step out of the ordinary into the supernatural realm of the living God. We are seated with God in Christ.

Although we are still walking in the earth physically, spiritually speaking, God raised us up with Christ and seated us with Him in the heavenly realms (Ephesians 2:6). 1st John 4:4 states: *"He who is in you is greater than he who is in the world"*, then 1st John 4:17 says, *"as he is, so are we in this world."* This means that we are seated in a position of tremendous authority, far above Satan, and all his principalities and powers of darkness.

We are children of God, and if children, then heirs of God, and joint heirs with Christ (Romans 8:16-17). An heir is a person legally entitled to the property or rank of another. An heir receives an inheritance because someone else did the work to acquire the fortune, and then died. Jesus did the work for us on the Cross. He died to pay our debt, then He rose again, victorious over sin and death. He inherited all God is, and all God has, and we got the inheritance with Him because He lives again, and we live in Him! Our inheritance in Christ is imperishable and eternal. It cannot be corrupted. This is an amazing blessing, but it is also a huge responsibility.

Many people say that God is in control. While it is true that God is sovereign, and has absolute power and authority, in the very beginning of creation, God gave dominion over the earth to man (Genesis 1:26). Look closely at these scriptures:

Psalm 115:16 in the Amplified Bible says, *"The heavens are the Lord's heavens, but the earth has He given to the children of men."*

Psalm 119:89 says, *"Forever O Lord, Your Word is settled in heaven."* God will not go back on His Word, and no one can thwart His Word (Isaiah 14:27, Job 42:2). He gave man dominion, so we are to rule over the earth. Ephesians 3:20 says, *"Now to Him who is able to do exceedingly abundantly above all that we ask or think, according to the power that works in us."* According to the power that works in us means God works with us and through us. Living the supernatural life requires intentional, whole-hearted devotion to the Lord and deeper intimacy with the Holy Spirit.

An inheritance has no value unless it is known and acted on. When we know what we have, who we are, and why we are here, we can by faith live supernaturally, just as Jesus did while He was on earth. Joint heirs do not act independently. We are to work with the Lord Jesus. We are called to be signs and wonders on the earth, and to be the light of the world and tell people about the love and redemption found in Jesus. We must take our authority as joint heirs with Jesus and declare God's Word in the earth.

I know that this is a lot to take in. So, I encourage you to meditate on these truths until you fully grasp the revelation of what you have, where you are, and who you are. Now, I'm not trying to say that we will never have another problem. Of course, we will. Our spirit is reborn. Our flesh is not. We must study God's Word to learn who we are in Christ and train ourselves to remember who we are. With our new life, we become high on Satan's hit list. When things come against us, remember that our identity is righteous. We must resist the devil and use our authority in the name of Jesus and the Word of God and send him away.

Remember, this is a process. As we stay connected to Christ and stay in the Word of God, we will become more like Jesus every day. As we learn who we are in Christ, we also learn to manifest our identity in Christ every day through our actions, words, thoughts, and activities.

Praying Through to Birth

*"You will keep in perfect peace whose minds are steadfast, because they trust in you."
Isaiah 26:3 (NIV)*

Out of the blue, the question came to me one morning, "Why did Jesus pray so much?" Do questions like this come to you? When they do, what do you do? Do you try to answer them yourself, or do you seek God for the answer? Do you remember when God asked Ezekiel, can these bones live? His answer was, "God, you know." Even if I think I know, if God asks, there must be something He wants me to see. So, my answer is, "God, You know." Show me what You want me to see.

Jesus was a man of prayer. In Mark 1:35-39, we see Jesus praying before preaching. He prayed before He committed Himself to the Father's care. He prayed for the needs of others. He worshiped and prayed prayers of thanks for God's provision, and He prayed for God's blessing on His ministry. My favorite prayer that Jesus prayed is found in John Chapter 17, where He intercedes for the disciples and all who would believe in Him because of their testimony (John 17:20). This prayer includes you and me today.

When Jesus prayed, He displayed complete confidence in the Father's perfect provision and plan. Like Jesus, we should pray about everything. Only God can bring wisdom in understanding of who He has created you to be. It is God who provides the strength and wisdom to fulfill our purpose. He calls us and directs us to work with Him in the earth. So, it is important to cover the entire process of birthing the Seed of Purpose in you with prayer.

Jesus said in John 4:34, *"My food is to do the will of Him who sent me and to accomplish His work."* He said in John 6:40, *"This is the will of my Father, that everyone who looks on the Son and believes in Him should have eternal life, and I will raise him up on the last day."* Above everything else we are sent to the earth to do our primary purpose is to do the will of the Father.

Jesus prayed, *"Not my will, but thy will be done"* because He desires that the Father's will be done above all else. This should be our desire as well, according to Matthew 6:33. When we pray, above everything else on our heart, we should pray that God's will may be done on earth as in heaven. That His name should be glorified, and His

Kingdom established. When we do this, everything we need for our journey will be added to us.

Jesus speaking directly to Peter said: *"31 And the Lord said, "Simon, Simon! Indeed, Satan has asked for you, that he may sift you as wheat. 32 But I have prayed for you, that your faith should not fail; and when you have returned to Me, strengthen your brethren."* (Luke 22:31-32). Jesus' prayer for Peter was for what was about to happen to him, as well as toward him fulfilling God's purpose for his entire life. Jesus has prayed for you. You should, in turn pray for others. Pray for God to complete what He's doing in their lives.

Relationship

Christianity is a relationship with God through Jesus Christ. Prayer is a conversation with God, as well as an encounter with God. Prayer is the primary way we grow and strengthen our relationship to the Father. Vision is usually given during prayer, and prayer is a vehicle through which a vision is fulfilled. Prayer is not just saying words, or repeating formulas, even if you pray prayers from a book like

Put the Word In Your Mouth. Real prayer comes from the heart of a person who believes what they are saying, even if they use a prayer book.

When we pray, we unleash a powerful force that cannot be stopped. Most of the time, I prefer to pray in tongues because when you pray in tongues, the Holy Spirit prays what's on God's heart, and your spirit is in direct contact with God. Paul encouraged the Corinthian Christians to speak in tongues in their individual prayer life as a means of spiritual edification or building up. In 1st Corinthians 14:14, the Bible says, *"He that speaks in an unknown tongue edifies himself."* Paul also continues in the same passage, *"For if I pray in an unknown tongue, my spirit prays."*

When people have a relationship, they want to spend time with each other, talk to each other, do things together, and learn each other's likes and dislikes. The more conversations and encounters they have, the closer they become. Parents want to spend as much time with their children as they can. Even when they become adults, we want to talk with them, see them and hear their voice. This is how

God feels about us, His children, and how He wants us to feel about Him.

Spiritual birth takes place the same way natural birth does. Just as a husband and wife's coming together intimately can result in the birth of a baby, intimacy with God brings forth God's will to the physical realm. By intimate, I mean, we must draw nigh to God, and seek Him with our whole heart. Intimacy does not come through prayer, but real prayer comes from true intimacy.

Peter prayed in 2 Peter 1:2, *"May grace and peace be multiplied to you in the knowledge of God and of Jesus our Lord."* Grace is God's unmerited favor. Peace is a gift from God and a part of His character. The peace that comes from God transcends circumstances. This peace is the security you need in the midst of turmoil. Apostle Paul wrote in 1st Thessalonians 5:23 *"Now may the God of peace himself sanctify you completely, and may your whole spirit and soul and body be kept blameless at the coming of our Lord Jesus Christ."* So, we can see why Satan does everything he can to rob you of your peace. If

God is peace, then to know God is to bask in His peace.

The more knowledge of God you get, the more you know Him and the more intimate you become with Him. With the knowledge and knowing of God, you receive multiplied peace and multiplied grace. Since God makes Himself known in His Word, reading your Bible every day is one of the best ways to grow closer to God. Spending time studying His Word, talking to Him about His Word, asking questions when we come across something we don't understand is going to draw you closer to the Lord.

You can make it fun by getting together with loved ones or friends and doing a Bible study. Or you can read a good daily devotional and then share your thoughts and understanding with each other. You will be surprised how your relationship with God and each other will grow. When you do this, you will find yourself growing spiritually and understanding of the depths and riches of God's love toward you (Ephesians 3:18–19).

> "*38 For I am sure that neither death nor life, nor angels nor rulers, nor things present nor things to come, nor powers, 39 nor height nor depth, nor anything else in all creation, will be able to separate us from the love of God in Christ Jesus our Lord."—Romans 8:38–39 (ESV)*

You begin to rest in His power and wisdom and actually see that He really does make all things work together for your good (Romans 8:28). I encourage you to let Him be your refuge. Develop a lifestyle of seeking His presence, and you will live in the peace of God. This is how we nurture our relationship with God.

> "*1 He who dwells in the secret place of the Most High shall abide under the shadow of the Almighty. 2 I will say of the Lord, "He is my refuge and my fortress; my God, in Him I will trust." —Psalm 91:1-2*

One thing we should remember is that God's purpose for the Seed of Purpose in us is to bring increase to the Kingdom of God. It is not for selfish gain. If our dreams and desires focus only on self-fulfillment, we will end up disappointed and unfulfilled when we achieve them. Scripture tells us that we must seek first the kingdom of God and His righteousness, above all else (Matthew 6:33).

It is God's desire for us to know the purpose He has embedded in us. As we get closer to God, He will share with us His vision, instructions and what to speak and pray to nurture the baby inside of us. We will receive divine guidance when we ask for it. I continue to hold on to a vision that God gave me during prayer years ago in my dining room. Over the years, this vision has encouraged me and given me staying power.

How do we pray to uncover the Seed of Purpose planted in us? "Delight yourself in the Lord, and he will give you the desires of your heart" (Psalm 37:4). This is not saying that we can treat God like a genie, that if we delight in Him, He will grant us whatever our heart desires. God wants us to incline our hearts toward Him. When the desires of our heart become the same as the desires of God's heart, then our prayers will align with God's will. And what we pray for will be something that God has already provided for us from before the beginning of time. He still may not answer when we desire, or the way we desire, because He knows much more about the present and future than us, and He will do what is best for us, and His plan for our lives.

Pray and pray often. Pray the way that is most comfortable for you. The most important part of prayer is that you seek God's voice and His answers. It has been said that our prayer life reveals the true state of our relationship with God. If this is true, what does this say about your relationship with God.

What about your relationship with God? Are you putting God first? Are you spending regular quality time with God and His Word? If not, think about what it would take for you to put God first in your life. Remember your prayers establish a relationship with the Father. Invest in your relationship. God wants to do many amazing things in the earth, and He looks for those willing to come in line with Him. Is there anything you have been shown that you need to change in order to get your life on the track God wants it to be? I encourage you to take the steps towards the change.

Fasting

Fasting and prayer is one of the most powerful spiritual combinations on earth. True fasting breaks the power of flesh, kills unbelief, and brings answers to prayer when nothing else works. According to the Bible, fasting is voluntarily reducing or eliminating your intake of food for a specific time and purpose. Jesus taught and expected His followers to fast, and He said that God rewards fasting.

In Matthew 6:16-18, Jesus said, *"...when you fast, do not be like the hypocrites, with a sad countenance. For they disfigure their faces that they may appear to men to be fasting. Assuredly, I say to you, they have their reward. But you, when you fast, anoint your head and wash your face, so that you do not appear to men to be fasting, but to your Father who is in the secret place; and your Father who sees in secret will reward you openly."* How many times have you talked with people and just out of the blue they let you know that they were fasting as if this makes them seem more spiritual? When I hear it, I'm like "Okay!"

In the Bible, God's people fasted for a number of reasons:

- Paul and Barnabas prayed and fasted for the elders of the churches before committing them to the Lord for His service (Acts 14:23).

- Nehemiah fasted, and prayed when he learned Jerusalem's walls had been broken down (Nehemiah 1:1-4).

- Moses fasted before he received the Ten Commandments (Exodus 34:28).

- Ezra declared a corporate fast and prayed for a safe journey for the nation of Israel they transitioned from Babylon to Jerusalem from (Ezra 8:21-23).

- Daniel fasted to receive guidance from God (Daniel 9:3).

- To prepare for ministry Jesus fasted 40 days and nights in the wilderness (Luke 4:2).

There are many more. Fasting helps you humble yourself in the sight of God, and transforms your prayer life. If you want to fast, do it by faith as your health allows it and God will honor your intentions.

"Yet even now," declares the Lord, "return to me with all your heart, with fasting, with weeping, and with mourning;" —Joel 2:12

The Battle For Your Purpose

"But for this purpose, I have raised you up, to show you my power, so that my name may be proclaimed in all the earth." —Exodus 9:16 ESV

There is an invisible world that is just as real as the visible world we live in. In this invisible world, a constant spiritual battle is going on between the Living God and Satan, and it has eternal implications. According to the Bible this spiritual battle started in heaven before the earth was created. This spiritual battle is spiritual warfare. As we draw closer to the return of Jesus, the war is increasing and becoming more intense as Paul warns in Second Corinthians 4:4.

> *"7 And war broke out in heaven: Michael and his angels fought with the dragon; and the dragon and his angels fought, 8 but they did not prevail, nor was a place found for them in heaven any longer. 9 So the great dragon was cast out, that serpent of old, called the Devil and Satan, who deceives the whole world; he was cast to the earth, and his angels were cast out with him."*
> —*Revelation 12:7-12*

Mankind was inducted into the battle in the Garden of Eden. The battle involves you because, as a child of God, you are a threat to Satan's kingdom. The closer you draw to Christ, the bigger the threat you are. So, the question is not, "Will I face spiritual warfare, but what do I do when it comes?" Understanding how to engage Satan and his demons in this battle is critical to experiencing the victory that Jesus has won for you. So, in this chapter, I'm going to be talking about spiritual warfare.

Most Christians have heard the term "spiritual warfare" at least once in their life, but many may not recognize it, or understand what it is, or what to do about it. Spiritual warfare is not a lot of what we've heard about. Much of what we see in the media is demonically inspired, and much of what happens in many churches is religious sensationalism.

Religious sensationalism and the media have made spiritual warfare and the supernatural seem silly, unbelievable, and spooky. This is part of Satan's tactic to deceive people into thinking he doesn't exist, to take our minds off who we are, and that spiritual attacks are not real, but simply things we have to endure as good Christians. Some people don't even believe that Satan and demons are real, and that's exactly what he wants, because then he and his demons can freely continue to deceive.

Some Believers see spiritual warfare as something that happens once in a while, whenever there is an issue or struggle in their life. But spiritual warfare is an ongoing war all Believers are involved in every day. If you are a Christian, you have experienced spiritual warfare and spiritual attacks. You may not have known what it was, or why things occurred, but it was part of the spiritual battle that we all are in.

You are pregnant with purpose, and Satan knows it. We don't have to look for the battle; it comes to us because of who we are. Each person's battle may be different. Your level of warfare may be different from another's, but every person will face some level of spiritual warfare. This will continue until Jesus returns. Satan cannot stop or block what God has called you here to do, but he can make you reject it. The war is between the Living God and Satan, but we have three enemies we contend with in this life: the world, our flesh (sin nature), and the devil. God has equipped us to deal with all three. Some people blame the devil and God for everything that goes wrong, but Satan, not God, is the source of evil.

Since I was a little girl, Satan has been trying to cause me to abort the Seed of Purpose inside me. I've endured things that no child or adult should ever endure. As I grew older, I gave my life to the Lord and began to draw closer to Him, and I sensed God was calling me to preach. When I told my mother God was calling me to preach, she said, "Ann, God doesn't call women to preach." I was young, and I admit I questioned the call after that for several years, until my pastor at the time confirmed the prophet's call on me.

I wrote the book "Put The Word In Your Mouth" almost twenty years before it was published. I had it on my computer's hard drive, and the technician who installed my internet destroyed it. Years later, God had me rewrite it and publish it. The book has helped many people to renew their thinking and speaking and change their life. That is what the enemy was trying to prevent, but he could not prevail because God has declared that the gates of hell will not prevail against the Church. You and I are the Church.

When I first accepted the call of God on my life, I had a very vivid dream where God warned me of an attack I was about to go through. In the dream, me and a group of Christians were in a hut in a village in Africa, supposedly to pray. Suddenly, there was a loud commotion outside. When I opened the door and looked out, I saw that we were surrounded by natives dancing around the hut and chanting some words that I could not understand, but I knew they were preparing to attack us. The whole scene seemed satanic.

When I turned to the people who were in the hut with me, they began to hurl accusations at me and say ugly things to me, and about me. I was shocked because I thought these people were my fellow Christians and friends. I was surrounded by the enemy outside, and I was in the midst of people who were working against me inside. I began to pray in the spirit (pray in tongues) and call on the name of Jesus. Suddenly, the natives and the people in the hut with me vanished.

Sure enough, it wasn't long before I began to endure an intense battle that my children and I still experience residue from. I have gone through some unbelievable battles, but the years following my daughter's passing have been the hardest so far. Satan did everything he could to destroy my character and even tried to kill me a couple of times. Despite it all, I continue to hold on to the promise God gave me as a young woman because I know in the end, it will manifest.

Many Believers have been taught that spiritual warfare is fighting against Satan, but spiritual warfare is not you fighting Satan to get victory. Spiritual warfare is simply you standing, proclaiming, and applying the victory that Jesus Christ has already won for you (1 Corinthians 15:57). A lot of people don't understand this, and they go about trying to beat the devil up, instead of standing in the victory they have. God has shown me how to walk in the victory that belongs to me. He has given us the tools we need to stand in the victory that Christ has won for us. Paul refers to them as the Whole Armor of God in Ephesians chapter 6:

"10 Finally, my brethren, be strong in the Lord and in the power of His might. 11 Put on the whole armor of God, that you may be able to stand against the wiles of the devil. 12 For we do not wrestle against flesh and blood, but against principalities, against powers, against the rulers of the darkness of this age, against spiritual hosts of wickedness in the heavenly places. 13 Therefore take up the whole armor of God, that you may be able to withstand in the evil day, and having done all, to stand.

14 Stand therefore, having girded your waist with truth, having put on the breastplate of righteousness, 15 and having shod your feet with the preparation of the gospel of peace; 16 above all, taking the shield of faith with which you will be able to quench all the fiery darts of the wicked one. 17 And take the helmet of salvation, and the sword of the Spirit, which is the word of God; 18 praying always with all prayer and supplication in the Spirit, being watchful to this end with all perseverance and supplication for all the saints"

So, truth, righteousness, the gospel, faith, salvation, the Word of God, and prayer are the tools God has given us to stand victorious against Satan's attacks and temptations. Paul says we are to be strong in the Lord's strength, not our own.

The Battle For Your Mind

Satan wants to control your soul. The soul is three parts: the mind, the will, and the emotion. Your mind is Satan's battlefield. This is where he uses lies to wage war against God's truth. Spiritual warfare attacks can look like:

- Thoughts of self-doubt.

- Depression, lingering grief.

- Loss of spiritual desire.

- Negative, disturbing thought life.

- Unusual dreams.

- Feeling discouraged, defeated, and depressed.

- Struggle with a lack of peace and feeling stress.

- Emotional wounds from the past continuously resurfacing.

- Heightened feelings of guilt, condemnation, shame, rejection, not belonging, and loneliness.

This list, though not exhaustive, shows us how the enemy attacks us in our mind. Put on and stand in the full armor of God (Ephesians 6:10-18). If you recognize that you are under attack, and Satan is using people to come against you, pray for them. Stand as an advocate before God for those whom Satan is using against you and bless them. I know it can be hard, but remember, Satan is trying to destroy them too. God can use you to deliver them out of his hands.

It's hard to stay angry with someone that you are fervently praying for. You don't have to pray for them in their presence. Go into your closet (your private place) and pray. They never even have to know, and God will reward you openly. Also, keep in mind that we do not fight flesh and blood, so remember who you are, and act accordingly. Use the

Word of God to stand and resist the enemy, and ask God to contend with him (Isaiah 49:25).

Understand that Jesus has already disarmed all principalities and powers and made a public spectacle of them, triumphing over them. (Colossians 2:15). So, when we stand on the Word of God, we are standing against the lie of Satan. No matter how it is presented, the lie of Satan has not changed since the Garden, that mankind can live independently of God, and be like God.

> *"For God doth know that in the day ye eat thereof, then your eyes shall be opened, and ye shall be as gods, knowing good and evil." — Genesis 3:5*

He convinced Adam and Eve in the Garden that they could be like God. He persuaded one-third of the angels in Heaven that they could become like God, and he continues to persuade many people today of the same lie. Jesus said Satan's only goal is to steal, kill, and destroy. He tries to discredit Christ, destroy your witness for the Lord, and make you abort your Seed of Purpose.

What is this Seed of Purpose I keep talking about? It is God's purpose for your life. When people respond faithfully to God's plan for their life, they thrive. When they embrace God's vision for their life, they find purpose and meaning.

Birthing the Seed of Purpose in you can only be done with the help of the Holy Spirit through the Word of God, and your obedience. The Bible tells us that once we get saved, we need to renew our minds with the Word of God. Most of what we've learned in the world has nothing to do with the ways of God. Renewing your mind to the Word of God is the most important thing you can do on your Christian journey. One of the reasons is that Satan's most effective battlefield is our mind.

> *"And be not conformed to this world: but be ye transformed by the renewing of your mind, that ye may prove what is that good, and acceptable, and perfect, will of God." —Romans 12:2*

Satan wants to convince you to live his lie. How you think, and what you think about, is vitally important in your life because the way you think is the way you live. Wrong thinking will lead to wrong believing. Wrong believing is going to lead to wrong living. Wrong living is going to lead to aborting your God given purpose.

If you allow yourself to be deceived in your mind, the fruit from that defeat shows up in your life. He especially targets us in our wounded areas, those places deep in our soul that carry pain from past hurts where strongholds have been built. He whispers lies in our conscious based on those strongholds.

A stronghold is a fortress where a power has control. These fortresses exist in our thought-patterns, opinions, and ideas. If hurtful words someone has spoken to you continue to run through your mind, and it feels like you have just been stabbed in the heart, there may be a stronghold there that Satan is using against you to stir up your emotions. Once our emotions kick in, we can find ourselves trapped in emotional turmoil, reacting, or overreacting to something that was planted by the devil. Imagine the joy this gives Satan. Strongholds can cause a believer to live in defeat.

Paul writes in Second Corinthians 10:3-6,

"3 For though we walk in the flesh, we do not war according to the flesh. 4 For the weapons of our warfare are not carnal but mighty in God for pulling down strongholds, 5 casting down arguments and every high thing that exalts itself against the knowledge of God, bringing every thought into captivity to the obedience of Christ, 6 and being ready to punish all disobedience when your obedience is fulfilled."

This passage makes it clear that there is a constant spiritual battle happening, and taking our thoughts captive is our primary defense.

Casting Down Imaginations

"Casting down imaginations and every high thing that exalteth itself against the knowledge of God, and bringing into captivity every thought to the obedience of Christ; and having in a readiness to revenge all disobedience, when your obedience is fulfilled" (2 Corinthians 10:5-6).

Every day we hear and see things that attempt to influence the way we think and see life. Many are lies sent to create doubt and lead us to wrong conclusions, causing us to question God's motives and faithfulness to us. Fighting a spiritual battle requires spiritual weapons. Praise the Lord, God has given us mighty spiritual weapons to pull down, demolish, or utterly destroy every stronghold that tries to keep us bound. So, we don't have to put up with strongholds, or be content to live with them.

Paul says that we need to cast down imaginations, reject every thought, idea, or view that does not line up with the knowledge of God. If it doesn't line up with who God is, or what God says, reject it, and stop thinking about it or meditating on it. Imaginations are pictures cast into your mind of thoughts, events, or conversations. They are not real. When you form a picture or an image of something that might happen and act on that image, you are acting on something that is not real.

Thoughts of sickness, failure, not being able to pay your bills, not moving in the power of God, etc. are images that the enemy wants you to exalt and receive. Reasoning can also be translated as imagination. Imaginations can also be translated as reasonings. There is no need to try to reason with Satan. Eve tried that, and we know what the outcome was.

Casting down imaginations and taking thoughts captive before they enter your heart and become a part of you is a spiritual warfare strategy to use against the enemy. You cannot fulfill your kingdom purpose if you receive the devil's thoughts that it cannot be done. If you accept what the devil is saying to you and about you, then you will receive the devil's results.

Victory is not about something you do, it is about what Jesus has done for you. Jesus is our example of obedience. We can bring our thoughts to the obedience of Christ by focusing on Jesus' obedience to the Father on the cross. Because of His incredible love for us, God sent Jesus to destroy the works of the devil (1 John 3:8). Then God gave us His word to renew our mind to the truth of who we really are, and what belongs to us. He sent us His Holy Spirit to help us think and act, and love like

Him. We must participate in His transformation process to experience all God has in store for us.

> *"Finally, brethren, whatever things are true, whatever things are noble, whatever things are just, whatever things are pure, whatever things are lovely, whatever things are of good report, if there is any virtue and if there is anything praiseworthy—meditate on these things." — Philippians 4:8*

Casting down imaginations of the enemy isn't something you do once, it must be done every day. *"Submit yourselves to God. Resist the devil, and he will flee from you"* (James 4:7). When you set your mind on the Spirit, your way of thinking will be transformed from being negative and destructive to positive and responsive to God's boundless love and grace. What you choose to trust and believe will affect every area of your life for either good or bad.

> *"Those who live according to the flesh set their minds on the things of the flesh, but those who live according to the Spirit set their minds on the things of the Spirit. For to set the mind on the flesh is death, but to set the mind on the Spirit is life and peace." —Romans 8:5-6*

No Weapon Will Prosper!

No weapon formed against you shall prosper, and every tongue which rises against you in judgment you shall condemn. This is the heritage of the servants of the Lord, and their righteousness is from Me," says the Lord. — Isaiah 54:17

This scripture basically says the fight we're involved in is a fixed fight. We win, no matter how hard the devil fights us. Tongues will rise against us, and what God has called us to do. No one likes being judged, criticized, or talked about, so how are we to react when things like this go on in our lives? When people intentionally hurt and come against us, how do we defend ourselves? Do we get mad and snap back?

Well, we know the attack is from Satan, the accuser of the brethren, and we know that whatever he says is a lie. The only way to combat and overcome a lie is with the truth. So, we declare the Word of God over the situation, you, and them to come against those accusations, and we pray for them. It may take some practice to get to the point where you can do this, because your old man may try to rise up. This is definitely not the right thing to do. So, if you find yourself in this situation, slow down, walk away, and submit to God. If you said or did something, you should ask God to forgive you, accept the forgiveness and keep moving.

If you are going through a trial or test, if the enemy is telling you that you will never come out of what you are in. He is a liar! Don't you dare give up! Satan does not have the power to keep you from birthing your purpose. No matter what comes against you, stay connected to the vine. Hold on to God's unchanging hand. Encourage yourself! Just as God brought Israel out of Egypt, Joseph out of the pit, the three Hebrew children out of the fire and Daniel out of the lion's den, He will bring you out of whatever you are in.

The battle will not last forever. If you follow God's leading, it will end, and when it does, you won't have to fight the same battle again. When Joseph was delivered from the pit, he never returned.

The three Hebrew children never returned to the fire. Daniel never returned to the lion's den!

Remember, *"Eye has not seen, nor ear heard, nor have entered into the heart of man the things which God has prepared for those who love Him"* (1 Corinthians 2:9).

Fight Spiritual Battles, the Jesus Way

The Bible assures us that the temptation to sin and disobey God is something we all encounter. In fact, First Corinthians 10:13 says, *"No temptation has overtaken you except what is common to mankind. And God is faithful; he will not let you be tempted beyond what you can bear. But when you are tempted, he will also provide a way out so that you can endure it."*

So, we are not unique in the temptations we experience. What we need to remember is that God will never allow a temptation to come to us that we cannot resist. He will always show us a way to escape it. So, it's not that temptation comes, but it is how we respond to it that's important.

Temptation is designed to make us fail. Satan and his demons continuously plot to make us fail (Ephesians 6:12). However, I don't believe that the Holy Spirit, who guides us into all truth, sits idly by and doesn't warn us of pending danger. I believe the Holy Spirit shows us the way out before the temptation, we just don't listen. So, when people say, "I fell into sin" or "God tempted me," I don't believe that's accurate. They did not heed the warning and walked right into trouble or sin. Scripture says, *"Let no one say when he is tempted, "I am being tempted by God," for God cannot be tempted with evil, and he himself tempts no one" (James 1:13 ESV).*

Some people will disagree with the statement that we don't have to sin, but truth is, sin is in our mortal bodies. Therefore, instead of it having power over us, we have power over it.

Let's look at Romans 6:8-12,

> *8 Now if we died with Christ, we believe that we will also live with him. 9 For we know that since Christ was raised from the dead, he cannot die again; death no longer has mastery over him. 10*

The death he died, he died to sin once for all; but the life he lives, he lives to God. [11] In the same way, count yourselves dead to sin but alive to God in Christ Jesus. [12] Therefore do not let sin reign in your mortal body so that you obey its evil desires. (NIV)

The Living Bible says it like this:

"[8] And since your old sin-loving nature "died" with Christ, we know that you will share his new life. [9] Christ rose from the dead and will never die again. Death no longer has any power over him. [10] He died once for all to end sin's power, but now he lives forever in unbroken fellowship with God. [11] So look upon your old sin nature as dead and unresponsive to sin, and instead be alive to God, alert to him, through Jesus Christ our Lord.

[12] Do not let sin control your puny body any longer; do not give in to its sinful desires. [13] Do not let any part of your bodies become tools of wickedness, to be used for sinning; but give yourselves completely to God—every part of you—for you are back from death and you want to be tools in the hands of God, to be used for his good purposes. [14] Sin need never again be your

master, for now you are no longer tied to the law where sin enslaves you, but you are free under God's favor and mercy."

So, before salvation, we were slaves to sin, but once we were saved, the power of sin was broken because Jesus gained the victory over sin, death, and hell through His death and resurrection. Sin is avoidable. The best way to avoid sin is to don't go into an area or situation where you will be tempted to sin (Romans 13:14). Jesus forgave the woman caught in adultery, but He told her to go, and sin no more (John 8:3–11). If it were not possible, He would not have said "sin no more." If you do sin, repent (turn away) and keep it moving.

When Jesus healed the man by the Pool of Bethesda (John 5:1–15), he later saw him and told him, *"See, you are well again. Stop sinning or something worse may happen to you."* When He said this, He was warning them against returning to a sinful lifestyle. If it were not possible, He would not have said stop sinning.

After John the Baptist baptized Jesus, He was led into the wilderness to be tempted by the devil.

"¹ And Jesus, full of the Holy Spirit, returned from the Jordan and was led by the Spirit in the wilderness ² for forty days, being tempted by the devil. And he ate nothing during those days. And when they were ended, he was hungry. ³ The devil said to him, "If you are the Son of God, command this stone to become bread." ⁴ And Jesus answered him, "It is written, 'Man shall not live by bread alone.'"

⁵ And the devil took him up and showed him all the kingdoms of the world in a moment of time, ⁶ and said to him, "To you I will give all this authority and their glory, for it has been delivered to me, and I give it to whom I will. ⁷ If you, then, will worship me, it will all be yours." ⁸ And Jesus answered him, "It is written, "'You shall worship the Lord your God, and him only shall you serve.'" ⁹

And he took him to Jerusalem and set him on the pinnacle of the temple and said to him, "If you are the Son of God, throw yourself down from here, ¹⁰ for it is written, "'He will command his angels concerning you, to guard you,' ¹¹ and

"'On their hands they will bear you up, lest you strike your foot against a stone.'" [12] *And Jesus answered him, "It is said, 'You shall not put the Lord your God to the test.'"* [13] *And when the devil had ended every temptation, he departed from him until an opportune time." — Luke 4:1-13 ESV*

The main point of the above passage is how Jesus dealt with temptation as a human. Jesus walked the earth as a man to show us what we are capable of doing. Luke says Jesus was filled with the Holy Spirit before He was led into the wilderness. The Holy Spirit is an incredible gift that God has given us to empower Believers to live like Jesus and be bold witnesses for the Gospel. You will not be able to walk this Christian journey or birth your Seed of Purpose without the help of the Holy Spirit. This is why Jesus said in John 16:7 that it was to our benefit that He would go away, so we would receive the Holy Spirit. Jesus walked the earth in the flesh as a man, but He lived according to the Spirit of God.

Jesus had just completed a 40-day fast, so He was probably good and hungry. Satan always attacks us when we are vulnerable. So, it is no surprise that he came to tempt Jesus in the area where He was vulnerable. But, as a man, Jesus had strengthened Himself through prayer and meditation on God's Word. And when the tempter came, He was ready, even though He was weak from fasting. Jesus knew going in that this was not a physical battle, but a spiritual one.

> *"For we do not wrestle against flesh and blood, but against principalities, against powers, against the rulers of the darkness of this age, against spiritual hosts of wickedness in the heavenly places." —Ephesians 6:12*

What this means is we cannot deal with spiritual things with physical things. Jesus used the Word of God to stand against Satan's temptations. Jesus said in John 6:63 that His very words are spirit, and they are life. When He was hungry after the fast in the wilderness, Satan tried to tempt Him to turn stones to bread, *"But he answered and said, It is written, Man shall not live by bread alone, but by every word that proceedeth out of the mouth of God."* (Matthew 4:4).

Hebrews 4:12 says, *"For the Word of God is alive and powerful. It is sharper than the sharpest two-edged sword, cutting between soul and spirit, between joint and marrow. It exposes our innermost thoughts and desires."* The Word of God is full of power. Jesus showed us the power of the Word, our authority and how to use it when He spoke to a tree and cursed it out loud saying *"Let no one eat fruit from you ever again."* The tree responded by dying from the roots.

In Mark 11:22-24 Jesus explained the authority and power of the Believer's words spoken in faith when he says *"Have faith in God. For assuredly, I say to you, whoever says to this mountain, 'Be removed and be cast into the sea,' and does not doubt in his heart, but believes that those things he says will be done, he will have whatever he says. Therefore I say to you, whatever things you ask when you pray, believe that you receive them, and you will have them."* Can you see that God has given us the authority to get His kind of results in every situation?

The Bible teaches us to have the mind of Christ (1 Corinthians 2:16). The only way we can have the mind of Christ is to study God's Word, believe it in our heart, and act upon it. When we pray the Word of God in faith, we get God's results! When we declare the Word of God in faith, we get God's results! When we say what we hear the Father say then God will perform what He spoke.

The three most powerful forces in the universe are always here to help us: God, the Holy Spirit, and Jesus. Like Jesus, we too must strengthen ourselves through prayer, reading, and meditating on the Word of God, so when the tempter comes, we will be armed and ready. We will know what the Bible says and how to wield its truth in our defense.

I have experienced many miracles standing on God's Word. I have walked through some horrendous battles by meditating and confessing specific Scriptures God gave me to stand on from my finished position in Christ! Be sensitive and obedient to what God is telling you to say and what not to say, and you will walk through every battle with excellence.

Angeline L. Williams

The Birthing Process

"For the vision is yet for an appointed time; But at the end it will speak, and it will not lie. Though it tarries, wait for it; because it will surely come, it will not tarry." —Habakkuk 2:3

As it is in the natural realm, so it is in the spiritual realm. In the spirit realm, there is no gender, so I am talking about both men and women in this analogy. Birthing the Seed of Purpose God has placed in you can be likened to bringing forth a child. Just as with a natural pregnancy, there is a time of conception and a time of birthing. Once the baby is conceived, it needs time inside the womb to grow and develop (usually nine months). Likewise, you and I must also carry the vision, the Seed of Purpose in our spiritual womb until its due season.

Conception and Implantation

When God does things, He begins with the end in mind. He said in Isaiah 46:10, *"I am the God who declares the end from the beginning ... My counsel shall stand, and I will do all my pleasure."* When He gives us a vision, it is usually the finished version, and it is usually beyond what we imagine or think we can accomplish. Then He gives us glimpses of His plan gradually, just as He did with Abram. God told Abram to look into the sky and count the stars. He said that his descendants would be as many as the stars of heaven and as many as the innumerable grains of sand by the seashore. Wow! That is a huge vision, isn't it?

Why would God instruct Abram to do this? Why does God give us glimpses of what His plan is for us? I believe He does this to get our imagination flowing and to spur our faith. Imagination is seeing. You cannot separate faith from the imagination. Imagination visualizes what faith knows to be true. We must see the invisible before we can do the impossible. To fulfill the purpose God has embedded in us, we will need to see it first, then believe it. Abram believed in God's power, but he had difficulty seeing the invisible and believing the impossible. Genesis 11:6 explains how powerful our imagination is.

> *"And the Lord said, Behold, the people is one, and they have all one language; and this they begin to do: and now nothing will be restrained from them, which they have IMAGINED to do."*
> *—Genesis 11:6*

This verse is showing an example of using our imagination the wrong way, that God is not pleased with. Hebrews 11:1 says, *"Faith is the confidence that what we hope for will actually happen; it gives us assurance about things we cannot see."* This is an example of using your imagination in way that pleases God. When our imagination is used this way, we see people and things the way God sees them.

Psalm 37:5 tells us, *"Commit your way to the Lord, trust also in Him, and He shall bring it to pass."* Proverbs 16:3 says it like this, *"Commit thy works unto the Lord, and thy thoughts shall be established."* Committing your way to the Lord means putting your entire life into God's hands. I love how the Amplified Bible Classic Edition translates Proverbs 16:3: *"Roll your works upon the Lord [commit and trust them wholly to Him; He will cause your thoughts to become agreeable to His will, and] so shall your plans be established and succeed."*

When I first moved to Atlanta, Georgia from Miami, Florida, I used to get lost all the time. Coming from a city with streets labeled with numbers and directions (south, north, east, and west) to a city where most of the streets are not, was a big change for me. In Miami, if I was on Northwest 27th Avenue and 163rd Street and I wanted to go down to 79th Street and 32nd Avenue, it was easy to navigate because the streets are numbered. In Atlanta, I would get lost most of the time because the streets are named, and I didn't know the city. When the GPS tracking systems came along, I ventured out much more.

When you are navigating unfamiliar territory, trying to get to a certain destination, you need something that will show you how to get there. Once you get there, you need to know how to get around to different places. This is what Psalm 37:5 is talking about. Commit your way to the Lord, let Him be your navigation, and He will get you there. We must learn to rely on God, not on ourselves or others, every step of the way, and then move in faith. So, God give us glimpses us more glimpses along the way as we relinquish control to Him, and faithfully move forward. Don't frustrate yourself trying to figure it all out.

God gave the Prophet Isaiah a glimpse of the peace and joy that Jesus' birth would one day bring to earth long before Jesus was born (Isaiah 7:14). Birth always begins with conception. If you can't conceive that God has placed a Seed of Purpose in you to do something amazing with your life, that He has a plan and a purpose for you, then you will never take the steps toward the life you are meant to live.

When God called the Prophet Jeremiah, He said, "Jeremiah, what do you see?" Jeremiah replied, "I see an almond branch." Then the Lord said, "You have seen well, for I am watching over my word to perform it" (Jeremiah 1:11-12) God was speaking to Jeremiah about things to come and assuring Him that what He saw will take place. You must believe God. Jesus says, *"It shall be done for you as you have believed"* (Matthew 8:13-NASB) Although we sometimes get a peek of what is to come, we still don't know all of what the future holds, other than in the end we win. We can hold on to that!

Proverbs 29:18 says, *"Where there is no prophetic vision the people cast off restraint, but blessed is he who keeps the law."* The word "vision" here refers to Divine communication as from revelation, prophecy, or a dream from God. Cast off restraint means "to ignore" or "neglect" God's Word and instruction (i.e., blessed is he who keeps the law). To birth what God has embedded in us we cannot lean to our own understanding, and way of doing things. Neither can we drop the vision. Since He knows the beginning, the in between and the end, it just makes good sense to follow His way.

The Holy Spirit Will Come Upon You

From the foundation of the world, God chose Mary, a woman who was promised in marriage to Joseph, to be the mother of the Son of God. When the appointed time came, God sent the angel Gabriel with a word, *"Hail, thou that art highly favored, the Lord is with thee: blessed art thou among women."*

When God wants to make us aware of the Seed of Purpose that He has planted in us, He gives us a word. With us today, it may not be an angel, but a prophetic word from one of God's prophets that aligns with an inward witness with our spirit. Or the Holy Spirit may speak through Scripture, and the word explodes in us, awakening what has been inside us all along, waiting on the appointed time. Or God may speak to our spirit.

The sight of Gabriel and the words he spoke to Mary frightened her, so the angel reassured her: *"Do not be afraid, Mary, for you have found favor with God. Behold you will conceive in your womb and bear a son, and you shall name him, Jesus."* What Gabriel said to Mary seemed impossible and she wondered how this could be since she was virgin, but he reassured her saying, *"The Holy Spirit will come upon you, and the power of the Highest will overshadow you; therefore, also, that Holy One who is to be born will be called the Son of God."* Mary responded, *"Behold the maidservant of the Lord! Let it be to me according to your word."* When God gives us a word we should respond like Mary, *"Let it be to me according to your word."*

The Seed planted in Mary was of the Holy Spirit. The Seed of Purpose planted in us is of the Holy Spirit as well. Godly purpose and vision do not come through human reasoning and imagination. If the purpose and vision that you see is not born of the Holy Spirit, it will be a work of the flesh, no matter how righteous it may seem. God does not anoint works of the flesh.

> *"And you shall speak to the children of Israel, saying: 'This shall be a holy anointing oil to Me throughout your generations. 32 It shall not be poured on man's flesh; nor shall you make any other like it, according to its composition. It is holy, and it shall be holy to you."* — Exodus 30:31-32

What do you see? Does it reveal God's holiness, glory, and power, and expose your human frailty? If God is the source of what you see, then you will clearly see that only God can fulfill it. Does it benefit the Kingdom of God? The vision of Jesus was centered on doing the work of the Father and meeting the needs of humanity. Your vision should be the same.

Finally, does it bring you fulfillment and peace of mind? The vision is easy to admire, but God did not give it to you for you just to admire it. He intends for you to live it. If your answer is "yes" to these questions, then continue to pray and follow God's direction. Notice that I keep encouraging you to pray about it and through it all.

Habakkuk 2:2 tells us to *"Write the vision; make it plain on tablets, so he may run who reads it."* Action and obedience go hand in hand. Run with your vision! Declare what God shows you. Act on what God shows you. You don't have to wait until everything lines up, until you know more, or have more. Do what you can with what you have now. Do what you know to be God's will now. Continue to pray and confess your faith. Even if you've told people about it and seems to be taking a long time, don't stop believing and don't stop declaring it. Fight unbelief with faith. God used people to declare the first coming of Christ for years, before He was born.

Just as Jesus, The Word, became flesh and lives among us, God wants His Seed of Purpose to become flesh in us. As our relationship with God develops, we begin to clearly see the Seed of Purpose God has planted in us. Then we must take that supernatural vision and nurture it by staying in the Word and in prayer. As we do, God gives us an unshakeable, unmovable desire to keep pressing towards that goal no matter how many setbacks occur.

Paul said we should be *"be steadfast, immovable, always abounding in the work of the Lord, knowing that your labor is not in vain in the Lord."* When He gives me a word to share in a book, all I can focus on until I complete it is meditating and studying the word, and writing down what He says.

During Pregnancy

A woman's body goes through physical, emotional, and mental stress while the baby is developing and growing inside her. Her body must stretch to accommodate the fetus as it grows, and there is nothing that she can do to stop it. If you've been pregnant or seen a pregnant woman, you know that for a stomach to stretch as much as it does is a miracle. We will also go through a stretching and molding, both mentally and physically, as the Seed of Purpose makes us ready for the labor process. We must make room for growth and expansion spiritually. The Holy Spirit may show us some things that are taking up space in our thoughts and hearts.

The stretching can seem sudden, or it can happen gradually over time. When I was pregnant with my first child, I did not show, and my stomach did not expand until I was in my seventh month. I went to sleep one night with a flat stomach and woke up the next morning with a huge belly. With my other two children, my stomach stretched gradually. We are like clay in the Potter's hand, we cannot control the process. Only God knows how long the process will last but following His instruction will help you get through it. God said He won't leave you or forsake you, and He won't. He will stay with you through the process.

God may stretch us beyond what we think is our limit to get us to our purpose. This stretching process can make you think you can't go any further, but like the skilled potter He is, God knows how to apply just enough pressure, and when to lighten up and give us a break. So, keep going. Don't abort your purpose or try to rush through the process. God is making you into a vessel that will display His glory to those around you.

Satan watches you being stretched, and he will do everything he can, and use every person he can, to prevent you from fulfilling your purpose. Every trial, every temptation, every affliction, and every setback are because of the Seed of Purpose in you. The good news is, regardless of how severe the attack is, it will not work! Again, I remind you that the battle has already been won! No weapon that forms against you shall succeed if you don't give up (Isaiah 54:17).

Satan thought he finally had Jesus cornered. He thought the cross would be the end for Him, but instead of an end for Jesus, it was a new beginning for everyone who puts their trust in Him (1 Corinthians 2:7-8). Just like with Jesus on the cross, what the enemy thought would destroy you, God is will use to deliver you, and propel you further into your purpose (Romans 8:28).

We don't like to go through the process because the stretching and molding is not comfortable. We want everything to be easy and immediate, but the process is necessary to prepare us for where we're going. Judas was a necessary part of God's redemptive plan. Trust God through the process. Even though at times it may not seem like it, He is with us every second of the day.

I've noticed that when I get a little discouraged or weary, something will happen to encourage me, or someone will come along to remind me why my purpose is so important. Everything is in His time, not ours. I have things written in my journal that God showed me in my thirties that are just now starting to be fulfilled in my life, and I am now in my sixties.

In 2018, I dreamed I was in a courtroom on trial. One by one, people that I knew came up and shared stories about me, most of which were lies. Each time someone stepped up to the stand because I knew them, I would think, finally, someone is going to tell the truth, but they just continued to tell lies. I would stand, protest, and say, "Your Honor, that's not true. They are lying."

My attorney would pull me down and say, "calm down Angeline. Everything is going to be all right. These lies won't stand." Finally, the judge asked me to stand for sentencing. He said, "Young lady I've heard all the testimony I want to hear against you, and I've taken it all into consideration, but I see something in you that the witnesses don't see, and I am going to base my decision on what I see and know to be true about you. Are you ready for your sentence?"

I really didn't expect a good outcome with all the lies that were presented, and I was nervous. In a court of law, a sentence can be a punishment for guilt or a vindication of one's innocence. I looked at my attorney and, with tears in my eyes, and fear in my voice and my head hung low, I said, "Yes, Sir, I'm ready." The judge then said, "Angeline Williams, I sentence you to greatness!" He banged his gavel and said, "Case dismissed!" I didn't exactly know what that meant, but it filled my heart with joy and hope.

Greatness is a status we all aspire to. To many people, greatness is about material possessions and accomplishments (power, money, and status). At first, I thought this was what God was saying in the dream. As I sought the Lord on the interpretation, I understood that sentenced, or destined to greatness in the Kingdom of God, means serving and blessing others. There is nothing wrong with material possessions and accomplishments.

In fact, God wants us to be great. He has endowed each of us with the resources that can certainly be used to bring these about, but He wants us to be great in His Kingdom! God's Kingdom is not measured by how many good deeds we've done, how many scriptures we can quote, what church we attend, or even how many souls we've won. Greatness in the Kingdom of God is serving and blessing others. Greatness in the Kingdom of God is not reserved for just a select few. Greatness (serving and blessing others) should be the identifying characteristic of every citizen in God's Kingdom.

This dream still brings unspeakable joy to my heart. This is one of those things that God does and uses to encourage me as I walk out my destiny. Many times, when my heart is heavy, the Holy Spirit speaks to me, "Hold on, you are destined for greatness." I very well might become financially wealthy and well-known, but that is not a big desire or concern of mine. If I had the money, I would purchase a couple of small apartment complexes or small motels and house battered women and children, and homeless families and help them get back on their feet.

God created you with seeds of greatness inside you. Negative things that happened in your past, and negative words spoken into your spirit, may have caused those seeds to lie dormant, waiting for Words of Life to water and nurture them and spring them into action. That is what happens each time the Holy Spirit brings this courtroom dream to remembrance. That is what happens when I study the Word of God with the Holy Spirit. Words of Life water and nurture the Seed of Purpose inside me and it grows.

I have no doubt that God wants you to succeed. If you are thinking that what God showed you hasn't happened in your life, I encourage you to hold on.

The Transition

As mentioned, there are four stages to the natural labor process. In a spiritual pregnancy, there can be several stages. The transition stage, when the baby moves into the birth canal in preparation to come into the world. After God gives us a glimpse of where He's taking us, the next part of the process is the transition, or wilderness. In the natural, it happens right before birth. This is the most painful part of pregnancy, and it can be excruciatingly painful. The mother's entire body becomes turbulent, and both the mother and the baby are at risk. The child, or the mother, or both, can die in the process. Rachel, the wife of Jacob, died in childbirth, but her son Benjamin survived (Genesis 35:16-18).

It's when a woman least expects it that her water breaks. So it is in the spirit realm. Unexpectedly, someone you love rejects you, a relationship is seemingly torn apart, or something happens, and you feel abandoned. Your heart is broken, and it seems that you just can't stop crying. Praise God! Your water has just broken in the spirit. Then the contractions come, and the labor begins.

If the mother delivers in the hospital, she might get an epidural if there is time. But, in the spiritual realm, there are no epidurals. So go through the travail. Let yourself feel what God wants you to feel. I know it is painful, but let yourself cry, but cry out to God and let Him cleanse you of anything that could harm your baby. Like natural labor, spiritual labor isn't easy, but it is worth it. John 16:21 tells us that a woman goes through the pain of birth, but once the baby comes, she forgets her pain because she experiences the joy of her newborn child.

When active labor begins, the mother's womb begins to open to make room for the child to come out. This, to me, is amazing! When God is ready for your purpose to come forth, He opens doors that no one can shut. He opens financial doors, ministry doors, prison doors, and people's hearts. He opens the windows and gates of heavens, and pours out of His treasures, and nothing can stop it! Things that seemed bound are released.

As excruciating as the pain is, the mother may feel the urge to push, but then she's told not to push. There may be problems with the umbilical cord, or shoulder dystocia, or some other complication. The doctor or midwife is trained to handle those such situations and do what is best for the mother and baby.

When birthing your Seed of Purpose, God tells us not to push in our own strength or wisdom, but to wait until He, by His grace, strength, and wisdom, says to push. Too early, or too late, we can harm the baby. Then, when everything is ready, through a great deal of determination, prayer, and faith, God says "push!" And something miraculous happens. Your baby comes to fruition. Most of the time, after all we've been through, when it happens, it seems sudden, and you can barely remember just how bad the struggle was.

Many things happen during the transition or wilderness stage. This is a place of preparation and revelation. As a babe in Christ, I was told that if things were not going right in my life, then I must be out of God's will. So, I thought because of the trials I was going through, I was out of God's will. After studying the exodus of the nation of Israel, I saw that God immediately took them into the wilderness after He delivered them from Egypt, rather than straight into Canaan.

In the Bible, Egypt represents the world. In these last days, we have got to let our dependence on the world go. The nation of Israel was in the wilderness for forty years. The older generation didn't make it out because of their ungrateful heart, stout words against God and disobedience. It is very important that we go through God's processes with humility. Most of us will have to learn humility as we go through, but we need humility to finish well, so keep a servant's heart, and wait on God.

God carried the nation of Israel into the wilderness to draw out the influences of Egypt from them. He wanted them to learn to lean on Him. This is the same reason He leads us into the wilderness. We need to learn to lean on Him and Him alone. The faith and the character we need to handle the promise and fulfill our purpose is developed in the wilderness. Remember, Jesus was driven into the wilderness also, but His experience ended differently (Mark 1:12).

Angeline L. Williams

Encouragement In The Labor Room

"Shall I bring to the [moment of] birth and not cause to bring forth? says the Lord. Shall I Who causes to bring forth shut the womb? says your God." —Isaiah 66:9 AMPC

From time to time we all need encouragement, especially when we have tried our best to do right and things go wrong. In those times we may become weary, but God always, somehow, gives you an encouraging word. Whether it is through something that we read, through something that someone says, through the Scriptures, or through a memory of how He brought you out before, God will not allow you to stay in a state of discouragement. Stand on the manna He sends you. Take it and apply it to your life.

There are many powerful stories of faith in the Bible that I turn to for encouragement. The stories of David, Joseph, and Caleb and the Parable of The Sower are ones that I particularly identify with. These stories confirm these three steps of the journey: the promise, the process and promotion. Let's look closely at them.

King David

King David was a shepherd boy who became King over Israel. The Israelites like many professing

Christians today, didn't like being a peculiar people, they wanted to be like everyone else. They wanted a king like the other nations (1 Samuel 8). God instructed Samuel to warn them of the disadvantages of a monarchy, but they insisted.

"19 Nevertheless the people refused to obey the voice of Samuel; and they said, "No, but we will have a king over us, 20 that we also may be like all the nations, and that our king may judge us and go out before us and fight our battles."

Saul was their choice. On the surface, he seemed like he would make a great king. He was strong and charismatic, and He seemed to have humility, but it wasn't genuine. He was impatient, distrustful, and determined to do things his way. God knew his heart, but He honored their wish and allowed the prophet Samuel to anoint Saul as king. After his first major victory, he built a monument to himself (1 Samuel 15:12). He disobeyed God, and God's spirit left him, never to return.

He sank deeper and deeper into depression and committed suicide by falling on his own sword. (1

Samuel 31). Have you ever been determined to have things your own way? I have. When I married my ex-husband, I went against what God had shown me. Things did not turn out well at all. I learned a valuable lesson, go with God no matter what your heart says.

God wanted Israel to have a king too, and David was His choice. God anointed him for the task even before he was ever crowned king. However, David was tormented by the jealous King Saul, who chased him for many years, trying to kill him. In the book of Psalms, we read about David's cries to God and his struggles.

Even as king, he made many mistakes, and struggled mightily with his flesh, but he was quick to repent, and he reverenced God. He turned to God for help and guidance in times of trouble. He prayed about his concerns. Apparently, prayer lifted him out of the pit of despair because in just about every Psalm ended with David praising God, even though nothing changed in David's surroundings.

King David was called a man after God's heart. It wasn't David's looks, stature, or natural talents, but his heart to repent, faith in, and obedience to God that made Him extraordinary. God works miracles through people who are willing to listen to Him and do what He says. If you can grab hold of this, and do whatever God says to do, you will find your life easier, and you will walk out your purpose. This is not about following a bunch of rules and regulations. It is about listening to the One who knows the very hairs on your head and the path He birthed you for.

There are times when I get a little tired standing in faith, but the Holy Spirit never lets me remain in this state for long. He always comes and reminds me of God's love and goodness, and I end up praising God and giving Him glory. In the midst of discouragement, you too will find your attitude shifting to praise rather than self-pity as you pour your heart out to God, and remind yourself of His great power, His faithfulness, and His love.

Joseph

What I love about God is that He can take the spiritual attacks and warfare we go through and work them for our good according to the purpose He has for us. Have you read the story of Joseph in the Bible? Joseph's brothers hated him because their father favored him. I don't think it's cool that a parent favors one child over the other, but in this case, I believe God has something to do with it. Joseph's story is another story of great encouragement for me.

When Joseph began to talk about the dreams God had given him, their hatred for him intensified. Satan used the jealousy in them to try to stop Joseph from birthing the Seed of Purpose God placed in him. Despite all he endured, he never lost faith in the promises of God. He believed God and followed Him no matter the circumstances, or the personal cost.

Joseph was called, but he was nowhere near perfect. He was a tattletale, and he bragged about his coat of many colors and his dreams and spoke down to his brothers. Clearly, some things needed to happen in Joseph's life before he could fulfill his purpose, so he had to go through a season of preparation (the wilderness).

The brothers took Joseph to the desert and threw him in a pit. The pit was on a road that the merchant caravans used on their way to the trading market. When the brothers saw the caravan coming, they took Joseph out of the pit and sold him to the merchants. God used this for Joseph's and his family's good.

So, Joseph is sold as a slave by his brothers, and he ends up serving in one of the King's officer's homes. The master's wife has the hots for him and approaches him every day trying to get him to do things with her. Every day he resisted her. One day, as Joseph resisted her attempt to lure him into her bed, she grabbed him by his coat and tried to force him. Joseph ran and left his garment in her hand. She got angry and falsely accused Joseph of having assaulted her, using his garment as evidence. Joseph was sent to the dungeon (Genesis 39:1-20).

The Bible says that God blessed Joseph while he was in prison. God gave him favor with the person in charge of the prison. Just like upstairs in Potiphar's home, Joseph was put in charge of everything in the prison.

So now he's in this dungeon and the cupbearer and the baker of the king of Egypt offended him, so he threw them in jail with him. These two men had a dream the same night, and they inquired of Joseph the meaning. Joseph interprets the dreams and proclaims God's faithfulness to the cupbearer and the baker. The chief cupbearer is restored to his position, but the chief baker is impaled, just as Joseph said in his interpretation. The chief baker forgets about Joseph, and he is chained in prison for two more years.

Pharaoh begins to have disturbing dreams. The chief cupbearer remembers the skill of Joseph and tells Pharaoh a man in the dungeon can tell you what the dreams mean. Joseph is called before Pharaoh and interprets his dream. Joseph told Pharaoh that it is God who provides interpretations and that he is merely the mediator (Genesis 41:16). Pharaoh recognized that God was with Joseph and promoted him to second-in-command of Egypt (Genesis 41:37-45).

Joseph was seventeen when his brothers sold him into slavery (Genesis 37:2), and thirty when he was released from captivity (Genesis 41:46). For thirteen long years, he held onto the dreams of leadership God gave him. He was convinced that He had a divinely ordained purpose and destiny, and that God would make it happen. He did not allow what he saw and experienced to defer him from what He knew to be true. That is the mindset and determination that we must have to birth the Seed of Purpose in us.

The reason I love this story so much is it shows that God truly does order our steps. It shows how the trials and tribulations we endure prepare us for the wonderful things that God has laid out for us in this life and the life to come. Joseph saw and believed his vision when he was a teen. They called him crazy, and it made the brothers angry, but the dreams God gave Joseph convinced him that he had a divinely ordained purpose and destiny. He held on to that throughout all he went through. Even though he was in the pit and prison, he was not discouraged because he knew what he saw was from God, and it would come to past.

A vision from God can sometimes make you look crazy because the end is so amazing, and even make some people angry. Once you've seen a vision from God, it takes over your life. If what you're seeing with your physical eyes is not what God showed you, then what you see is temporary. Continue to believe God until you see what was revealed to you. This story teaches me humility, and not to complain against God's plan and process.

The Bible is filled with people who endured many struggles and setbacks before their purpose was realized. When you find yourself getting discouraged, go to the story of Jacob, who worked 14 years for Rachel (Genesis 29). Or to the story of the widow Ruth, who went from being homeless and working in a field picking up scraps to owning the field (the Book of Ruth). In the New Testament, Peter went from leader to failure to leader again. Paul was a Pharisee bent on persecuting Christians. Then he had an encounter with Jesus on a Damascus Road and went on to start many churches and write much of the New Testament. There are many more. Just open your Bible and read.

It's Going To Be Alright

I used to wonder why I've had to endure so many traumatic circumstances in my life. I didn't wonder about the ones that I caused, but I wondered about the circumstances that I had no control over. I wondered why people would gravitate to me, and out of the blue share their life story and problems with me. I would see myself in them and would try to comfort and encourage them, and pray for them. I finally realized that God was using the pain I have endured to plant seeds of hope in others. Seeds that could help bring them out of the pit of pain that they were in.

There's a saying I often hear, "If it wasn't for the bad times, I wouldn't know how to enjoy the good times." Until Jesus comes, we will all have some bad times. God used David and Joseph's wilderness experience to developed the character in them they needed to handle the promise He had embedded in them. He does the same with us. You have been called to greatness, but you must go through the wilderness, your season of preparation, so humble yourself and go through the process. God will be faithful to you in whatever wilderness you are facing, just as He was with David and Joseph.

The Word of God says all things work together for good to them that love God, to them who have been called according to His purpose (Romans 8:28). I don't know how He does it, but God in His wisdom and love takes the bad, the sad, and the evil things that touch our life, and works them together for good for us, and for the Kingdom. God is amazing!

I also believe God in His wisdom allows some things to happen for our growth because, like table salt, they are necessary for life. Jesus taught this concept in Matthew chapter five when He said, *"Ye are the salt of the earth... Ye are the light of the world... Let your light so shine before men, that they may see your good works, and glorify your Father which is in heaven."*

We cannot live without some salt in our bodies and light in our lives. Likewise, the world needs salt and light. Both salt and light have properties that affect things around them. Table salt is made up of sodium and chloride. Sodium by itself is a deadly poison, and chloride by itself is a deadly poison also, but put them together, and you have table salt. Table salt is used as a preservative to enhance flavor, and as a healing and cleansing agent. Believers in Christ, by their very presence in the world, help preserve the world, and hold back the wrath of God.

It may seem that evil is running rampant today, but imagine a world without Believers praying and decreeing Thy Kingdom come. Thy will be done. There would be nothing to hold back the evil that's trying to take over the world. God has intercessors on the wall who are constantly praying for His will and purpose on earth, and the prayers of the righteous are very powerful. Just as salt has a positive influence in the world, light has a tremendous influence as well. Believers in Christ are to influence the world by putting our light forth, living an active faith, and letting the world know that we serve a tangible, living God.

The circumstances we encounter are opportunities to shine brightly for the Lord and to share God's overcoming truth with those around us. Your family and community can tell what you believe by how you live. Some of them may try to attach your past to who you are today, just as they did with Jesus. Stay focused. This is a tactic of Satan to distract you from your God-given purpose. Keep it moving. Be who God says you are.

I'm reminded of a phone call I received from someone I allowed to live with me years back. Because they were family, I reluctantly allowed this person to live with me three times, but each time the results were not good. The call came at a time when I was under heavy enemy attack. Everywhere I turned, I was being accused of something that I did not do or reminded of past mistakes. That day, the battle was intense, and I was feeling pretty low. During the call, this person began to accuse me of being the reason that they were not in a wealthy place in their life. They said, "You didn't give me a chance."

"I actually gave you three chances, and gave you Christ," I responded. They continued with the accusation. Satan uses tactics like this to get into your mind and plant guilt and condemnation because he knows that guilt and shame are very destructive to our relationship with God. Shame and guilt are based on deception, even if what someone says about your past is true. That is who you used to be.

> *"Therefore, if anyone is in Christ, he is a new creation; old things have passed away; behold, all things have become new." — 2 Corinthians 5:17*

> *"There is therefore now no condemnation to those who are in Christ Jesus, who do not walk according to the flesh, but according to the Spirit." —Romans 8:1*

Never forget that Satan is a wolf who comes in sheep's clothing. He is diabolical and only comes to steal, kill, and destroy. He will do all he can to agitate, disturb, perplex, and confuse you, and he will use whoever will yield to him, even your own children. He knows that if you focus and meditate on the trouble, you will lose your focus on what God said. When you are no longer focused on what God said, the trouble you are facing becomes more real to you than the Word God spoke.

This person called, supposedly with good intentions, but Satan's goal was to get me to abort my baby and abandon the vision, the prophetic word, that God has placed over my life. Because of the love I have for the person, I listened, thinking they just needed to get things out, so they could move on. As the accusations went on, I admit, I began to wonder if I had been fair. Then, visions of Eve in the Garden trying to reason with Satan ran through my mind, and I realized what was happening, and I got off the phone.

Sometimes you are just going to have to love people on your knees and let God work things out until you can come together. Stay alert, for we do not wrestle against flesh and blood, but against principalities, against powers, against the rulers of the darkness of this age, against spiritual hosts of wickedness in the heavenly places (Ephesians 6:12). Hallelujah, I thank God that He loves us so much that He will not leave us to the wolves.

Holy Spirit reminds us *"Rejoice highly favored one, the Lord is with you; blessed are you...and blessed is the fruit of your womb!"* (Luke 1:28, 42) Rejoice highly favored one, the Lord is with you.

Final Thoughts

In everything give thanks; for this is God's will for you in Christ Jesus. —1 Thessalonians 5:18

So, after reading the message, do you have an idea of what your Seed of Purpose is? Does it look what you have been sensing? I remember as a young girl I would write poetry and letters to God as a way of escaping the traumatic environment I was in. I have always been a loner, and didn't have many friends. Writing always took me to another place.

Even though I spent much of my time writing, I never dreamed that I would become an author or help others become authors, and I definitely didn't think I would become a preacher. I was going to get married and become a lounge singer by evening, and a journalist by day. That was my plan. Someone once said if you want to make God laugh, tell Him your plans. I see now how my purpose always presented itself. I just didn't pay attention.

I tried to follow my plan and enrolled in college with a journalism major. I was a young single parent, and I needed to get a job to take care of my children. I quit college to get a job. My first job was as a maid at the Fontainebleau Hotel on Miami Beach. My dad came around and convinced me to go back to school. I enrolled in trade school to learn graphic arts and printing. It was quicker to complete than a degree in journalism, which was my reasoning.

My dad and his fiancé kept my kids while I went to school. I excelled and loved what I was doing. I worked at newspapers, magazines, and printing companies as a typesetter, proofreader, editor, and layout artist. I loved what I was doing. I would get wrapped up in the work, and it didn't feel like work. I look back now and see how God ordered my steps to get me here.

This is how God led me to birth the Seed of Purpose He placed in me. Has something similar happened to you? If you still don't know what your purpose is, ask God to reveal your purpose to you. *"Ask, and it will be given to you; seek, and you will find; knock, and it will be opened to you. For everyone who asks receives, and he who seeks finds, and to him who knocks it will be opened"* (Matthew 7:7-8). When God reveals it, be willing to pay the price for the fulfillment of your God-given purpose.

You are unique. Your calling may look much different from mine. Maybe you get excited about starting a new business or helping people find jobs. Maybe you're called to be a Christian play writer or act in them. Maybe you are called to be an honest car mechanic or car salesman. Maybe you are called to be a great teacher and help the next great inventor make it through school. Whatever your purpose is, it will feel like it's a part of you, and over the years, God has been ordering your steps to the spiritual labor room.

Listen to your dissatisfaction. If you've been miserable at your job for a long time, and you've been praying for a way out, maybe God has another plan for you.

Listen to what others are saying. Have countless people suggested that maybe God wants you to do this or that? God may be trying to tell you something through them. Yes, there are times when we shouldn't listen to what others say. But if what they say agrees with your passions, inner convictions, gifting and what God has already revealed to you, it may be an indication of your Seed of Purpose.

Listen to your gifts. I've always loved English, but hated math. Remember, I loved writing. What do you love to do? What are your gifts? Consider your talents and gifts. They may be road signs to where God is leading you.

Again, I say pray. Ask God what your purpose is. He wants you to discover His purpose for you. Remember, your purpose is not just about you reaching a goal; it is about fulfilling God's desire for your life. It's about what God wants to do through you. It is for the Kingdom. Trust that since God has called you, He is able to reveal your purpose to you as you diligently seek Him. Step into what God is calling you to with tenacity because you know the Mighty and Faithful God has your back!

Don't confuse your assignment with your purpose. You will have many assignments on your way to birthing your purpose. Whether good or bad, see every phase in your life as a stepping stool into your purpose. Keep going, God's grace will get you to the other side. Keep in mind that it's not where you are, but how you think and act, and what you do where you are. Remember, you are participating in God's divine, eternal purposes. Again, God's priority is people, and your purpose will be a reflection of His heart to reach someone. Measure your success by the fruit that follows.

Nothing we do in Him can ever be diminished or destroyed because He alone is the source and the power. You may doubt the Lord from time to time. However, Jesus knows that you're going to produce fruit because He has chosen you!

There is so much more that I would love to share that will help you walk in the victory of Christ, so I invite you to follow me on my blog at:

- www.angelinelwilliams.com.

- Facebook: www.facebook.com/angeline.williams

- or Twitter: twitter.com/MsAngelineW

About The Author

Prophetess Angeline L. Williams is an author, speaker, Bible teacher. She has accepted her assignment to speak the truth with boldness and transparency. She was licensed and ordained in 2002 to preach the Gospel. She is a submitted vessel of God who flows in the ministry gifts of prophet, evangelist, and teacher.

Her passion for God and His Word has led to an anointing to preach and teach the Word of God with authority, revelation, and deliverance. Her messages are illuminated with revelation, personal testimony and a depth of wisdom, and insight resulting from decades of study, and relationship with God.

She is also the author of three other bestselling books: Put The Word In Your Mouth: Believe God, Agree With His Word, Declare His Word, and Change Your Life, I Don't Believe in Fairytales: Breaking Anti-Marriage and Promises, Promises. God Always Keeps His Promises.

She is the owner of Williams DocuPrep, where she has been providing self-publishing services to authors, and independent publishers since 2005. Visit her website at www.williamsdocuprep.com to learn more.

Prophetess Angeline is available to speak at churches, groups, conferences, workshops, or any place God opens a door. Contact her about speaking at your event at: www.angelinelwilliams.com

Other books by author available online where books are sold.

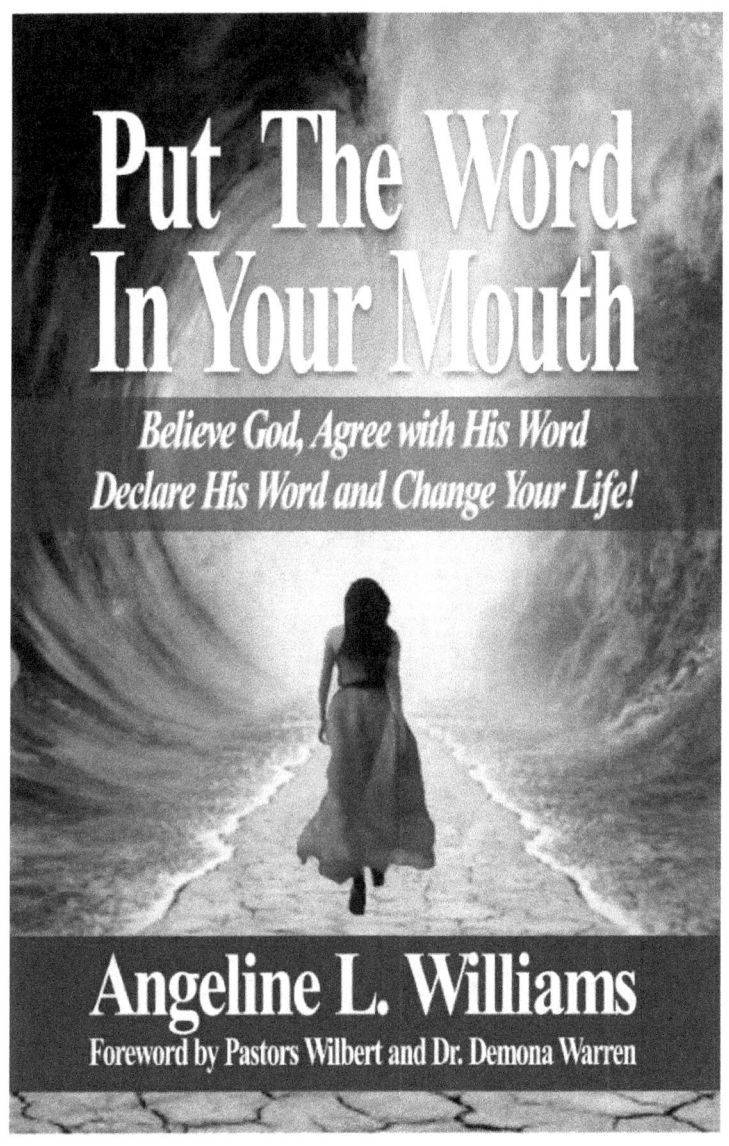

www.ingramcontent.com/pod-product-compliance
Lightning Source LLC
Chambersburg PA
CBHW071848070526
44583CB00016B/1591